Living as Global Citizen

An Introduction to the Sustainable Development Goals

地球市民として生きる：英語で学ぶ SDGs 実践入門

Kazuya Oseki　Kevin M. McManus

南雲堂

NAN'UN-DO

Living as Global Citizens
An Introduction to the Sustainable Development Goals

by
Kazuya Oseki
Kevin M. McManus

The content of this publication has not been approved by the United Nations and does not reflect the views of the United Nations or its officials or Member States.
United Nations Sustainable Development Goals website: https://www.un.org/sustainabledevelopment/

The contents of this textbook are based on available information as of November 2020.

Download Audio
音声ファイル
無料 DL
のご案内

このテキストの音声を無料で視聴（ストリーミング）・ダウンロードできます。自習用音声としてご活用ください。
以下のサイトにアクセスしてテキスト番号で検索してください。

https://nanun-do.com　テキスト番号［ **512116** ］

※ 無線 LAN（WiFi）に接続してのご利用を推奨いたします。

※ 音声ダウンロードは Zip ファイルでの提供になります。
お使いの機器によっては別途ソフトウェア（アプリケーション）の導入が必要となります。

Read by

Hannah Grace（アメリカ英語）
Josh Keller（アメリカ英語）

※ Living as Global Citizens 音声ダウンロードページは以下の QR コードからもご利用になれます。

A Message to Learners

This unique textbook has been designed not only to improve your English language ability but also to enable you to begin the journey toward becoming a global citizen.

The concept of global citizenship is based upon the idea that every single one of us is a member of the global community, and that we all have the power—collectively and individually—to make the world a better place. This textbook will introduce you to the Sustainable Development Goals, which were established by the United Nations General Assembly in response to the most serious problems facing the world today. You will learn about the practical things you can do to help solve these problems as the textbook guides you through a process of *making connections*, *recognizing differences*, and *looking to the future*. It’s an exciting journey, and one that will ask you to reflect upon and develop your own values as you go. You might even think of it as two distinct life-changing journeys: one an "outer journey” to learn more about our complex world, and the other an "inner journey" to learn more about yourself.

Our hope is that, in years to come, you will be able to look back upon this textbook and remember it as your first step toward becoming a global citizen and creating a more sustainable, better world.

Kazuya and Kevin

Special Thanks

We would like to thank the two wonderful students who contributed greatly to this textbook: Ms. Satsuki Yamagata, who created the beautiful hand-drawn flower images throughout the book as well as the scene depicted on the inner cover, and Ms. Ayano Uchiyama, who added color to each chapter with her original graphs and illustrations.

About This Textbook

This textbook will help you improve your English skills in an interesting and engaging way while also gaining a better understanding of global issues. Each of its fourteen chapters consists of the following components:

Chapter 1

Global Perspectives

Introduction

1. Have you ever heard of "SDGs"? What do you think the three initials stand for?

2. The SDGs are a set of seventeen goals which, if achieved, will make the world a better place. If you could change anything to make the world a better place, what would you change? Why?

SUSTAINABLE DEVELOPMENT GOALS

1 NO POVERTY

10 REDUCED INEQUALITIES

13 CLIMATE ACTION

10

Introduction

Every chapter begins with a large color picture and a pair of thought-provoking questions relating to the chapter's theme as explored in the main reading passage.

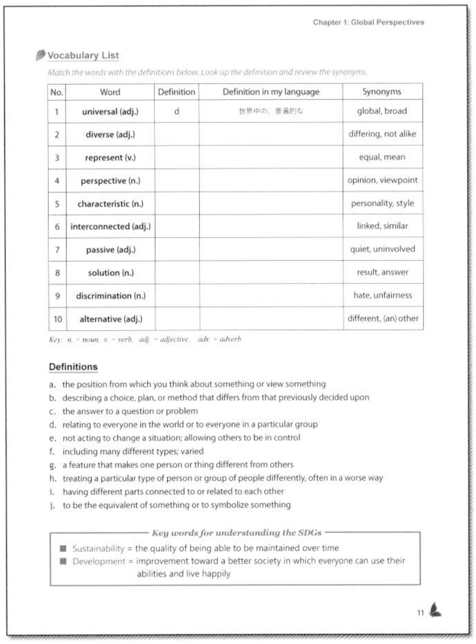
Chapter 1: Global Perspectives

Vocabulary List

Match the words with the definitions below. Look up the definition and review the synonyms.

No.	Word	Definition	Definition in my language	Synonyms
1	universal (adj.)	d	世界中の、普遍的な	global, broad
2	diverse (adj.)			differing, not alike
3	represent (v.)			equal, mean
4	perspective (n.)			opinion, viewpoint
5	characteristic (n.)			personality, style
6	interconnected (adj.)			linked, similar
7	passive (adj.)			quiet, uninvolved
8	solution (n.)			result, answer
9	discrimination (n.)			hate, unfairness
10	alternative (adj.)			different, (an) other

Key: n. = noun, v. = verb, adj. = adjective, adv. = adverb

Definitions

a. the position from which you think about something or view something
b. describing a choice, plan, or method that differs from that previously decided upon
c. the answer to a question or problem
d. relating to everyone in the world or to everyone in a particular group
e. not acting to change a situation; allowing others to be in control
f. including many different types; varied
g. a feature that makes one person or thing different from others
h. treating a particular type of person or group of people differently, often in a worse way
i. having different parts connected to or related to each other
j. to be the equivalent of something or to symbolize something

Key words for understanding the SDGs

- Sustainability = the quality of being able to be maintained over time
- Development = improvement toward a better society in which everyone can use their abilities and live happily

11

Vocabulary List

Students acquire new vocabulary through a word-definition matching activity. Each new vocabulary item is presented alongside synonyms using words that students will likely already know.

Reading Preview

The matching activity at the beginning of every reading passage encourages students to preview the passage by scanning the text for keywords and concepts represented by the pictures.

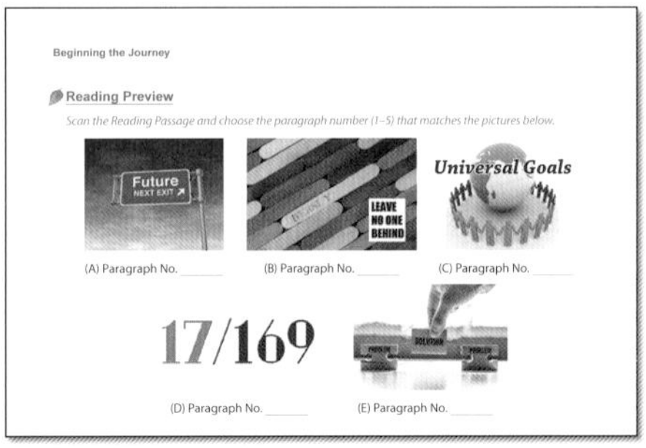
Beginning the Journey

Reading Preview

Scan the Reading Passage and choose the paragraph number (1–5) that matches the pictures below.

(A) Paragraph No. ______ (B) Paragraph No. ______ (C) Paragraph No. ______

(D) Paragraph No. ______ (E) Paragraph No. ______

Reading Passage

Common Goals for the Future

DL 2

[1] The Sustainable Development Goals (SDGs) are a set of universal goals to make a better world. All of the member states at the 2015 United Nations General Assembly agreed upon them. The SDGs clarified the global challenges that both developed and developing countries need to tackle in three areas: the environment, society, and the economy. Importantly, these goals were not simply created by government organizations but also by a diverse range of groups including companies, NPOs, minorities, and young people. The SDGs represent everyone and are based on the collective voices of people from around the world.

[2] The SDGs aim to change our future and reflect a vision of our world in 2030. They are made up of seventeen goals and 169 targets for achieving them. Each goal focuses on a different important issue such as climate change or poverty. It may seem impossible to tackle so many different problems on such a large scale. However, if we view the SDGs from "global perspectives," we can see that they all share certain characteristics. Let's take a look at three key perspectives and how they relate to the SDGs.

[3] The first perspective is *making connections*. All of the goals outlined in the SDGs are interconnected with each other. This means that rather than trying to tackle all seventeen goals at the same time, we can start with one and use it as a gateway for dealing with other issues. The problems facing our world are very complex, so we first need to understand how they are related to each other on a global scale. We also need to be aware of how they connect

Chapter 1: Global Perspectives

with our daily lives. In other words, in order to solve the world's problems, we cannot think of ourselves as passive outsiders. Instead, we should take daily steps toward a solution.

[4] The second perspective is *recognizing differences*. The SDGs aim for a world without discrimination in which "no one is left behind." They take a holistic approach in which everyone from you and me to different vulnerable groups, animals, and even the environment is included. To achieve this, we should try to accept diversity and recognize that there is more than one perspective on any single issue. There is no single "right answer" to any of the problems identified by the SDGs. Different possible answers will be created as we tackle the world's biggest problems together.

[5] The final perspective is *looking to the future*. According to the SDGs, just learning about the issues is not enough. To change the world, we need to reflect on our own individual lifestyles and values. The problems we are facing are difficult to overcome, so people from different backgrounds must come together to work toward their common goals. The future is not set in stone. There are many possible alternative futures depending on the actions we take today. Even if we choose to do nothing, it will still affect our common future.

Reading Passage

Reading passages are accessibly written, include interesting and surprising facts, and colorfully highlight target vocabulary. Each passage applies the following five-paragraph structure:

- Paragraph 1: Introduction
- Paragraphs 2 and 3: Discussion of a global issue
- Paragraph 4: Discussion of how the issue relates to Japan
- Paragraph 5: Suggestions regarding everyday actions to help solve the issue

Check Your Understanding

Reading passages are followed by four comprehension questions. Two of these questions are open-ended and check the students' comprehension of general concepts. The remaining two questions check specific details from the passage.

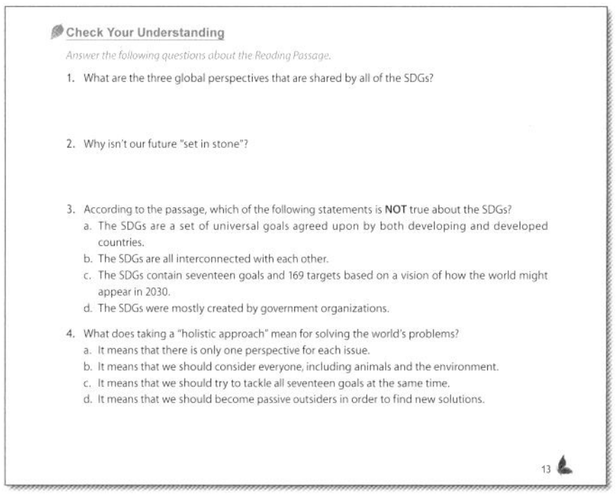

Check Your Understanding

Answer the following questions about the Reading Passage.

1. What are the three global perspectives that are shared by all of the SDGs?
2. Why isn't our future "set in stone"?
3. According to the passage, which of the following statements is **NOT** true about the SDGs?
   a. The SDGs are a set of universal goals agreed upon by both developing and developed countries.
   b. The SDGs are all interconnected with each other.
   c. The SDGs contain seventeen goals and 169 targets based on a vision of how the world might appear in 2030.
   d. The SDGs were mostly created by government organizations.
4. What does taking a "holistic approach" mean for solving the world's problems?
   a. It means that there is only one perspective for each issue.
   b. It means that we should consider everyone, including animals and the environment.
   c. It means that we should try to tackle all seventeen goals at the same time.
   d. It means that we should become passive outsiders in order to find new solutions.

13

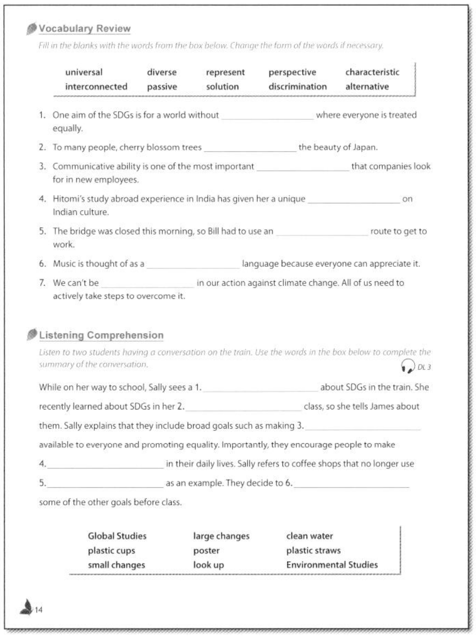

Vocabulary Review

Fill in the blanks with the words from the box below. Change the form of the words if necessary.

universal	diverse	represent	perspective	characteristic
interconnected	passive	solution	discrimination	alternative

1. One aim of the SDGs is for a world without ________ where everyone is treated equally.
2. To many people, cherry blossom trees ________ the beauty of Japan.
3. Communicative ability is one of the most important ________ that companies look for in new employees.
4. Hitomi's study abroad experience in India has given her a unique ________ on Indian culture.
5. The bridge was closed this morning, so Bill had to use an ________ route to get to work.
6. Music is thought of as a ________ language because everyone can appreciate it.
7. We can't be ________ in our action against climate change. All of us need to actively take steps to overcome it.

Listening Comprehension

Listen to two students having a conversation on the train. Use the words in the box below to complete the summary of the conversation.

DL 3

While on her way to school, Sally sees a 1.________ about SDGs in the train. She recently learned about SDGs in her 2.________ class, so she tells James about them. Sally explains that they include broad goals such as making 3.________ available to everyone and promoting equality. Importantly, they encourage people to make 4.________ in their daily lives. Sally refers to coffee shops that no longer use 5.________ as an example. They decide to 6.________ some of the other goals before class.

Global Studies	large changes	clean water
plastic cups	poster	plastic straws
small changes	look up	Environmental Studies

14

Vocabulary Review

Rather than follow the vocabulary list, this sentence-matching exercise comes *after* the reading and comprehension activities. This is to encourage spaced repetition of the new vocabulary items, thus facilitating acquisition.

Listening Comprehension

Each chapter includes a short conversation between two speakers, followed by comprehension questions. The conversations refer to real-life actions that may be taken in order to relieve the problems explained in the reading passage.

SDG Highlight

This section highlights a Sustainable Development Goal relating to the contents of the reading section and the listening section.

Making Connections / Recognizing Differences / Looking to the Future

This section facilitates the development of global perspectives by requiring students to reflect upon the current chapter and express what they learned. The questions are designed to encourage relational thinking and provide the basic framework for oral interaction with classmates.

Action

This section encourages students to proactively take steps to help solve the problems under discussion by further deepening their understanding, and by making changes in their daily lives.

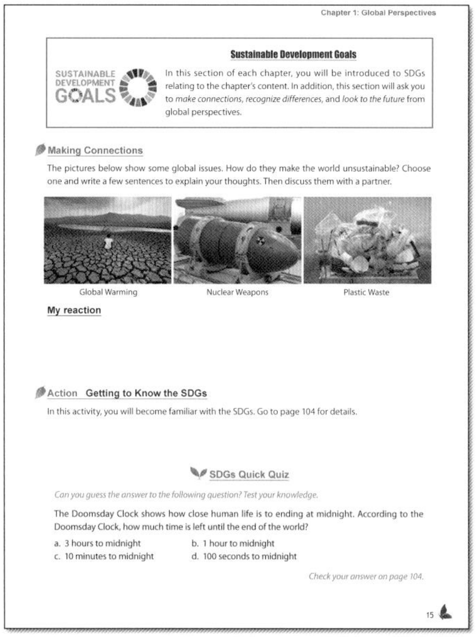
Chapter 1: Global Perspectives

Sustainable Development Goals

In this section of each chapter, you will be introduced to SDGs relating to the chapter's content. In addition, this section will ask you to *make connections*, *recognize differences*, and *look to the future* from global perspectives.

Making Connections

The pictures below show some global issues. How do they make the world unsustainable? Choose one and write a few sentences to explain your thoughts. Then discuss them with a partner.

Global Warming | Nuclear Weapons | Plastic Waste

My reaction

Action Getting to Know the SDGs

In this activity, you will become familiar with the SDGs. Go to page 104 for details.

SDGs Quick Quiz

Can you guess the answer to the following question? Test your knowledge.

The Doomsday Clock shows how close human life is to ending at midnight. According to the Doomsday Clock, how much time is left until the end of the world?

a. 3 hours to midnight
b. 1 hour to midnight
c. 10 minutes to midnight
d. 100 seconds to midnight

Check your answer on page 104.

15

SDGs Quick Quiz

This section consists of interesting "quiz-style" questions relating to the highlighted SDG. Students are encouraged to take a guess based on their existing knowledge rather than looking up the answer online.

Chapter 1 Action Worksheet

Getting to Know the SDGs

Step 1 Look at each of the seventeen SDGs below and divide them into three groups: *Environment*, *Society*, and *Economy*. There is no single correct answer, so use your imagination.

Environment	Society	Economy

Step 2 Share your opinion with a partner.

Step 3 Select three of the SDGs that interest you the most and write down why you chose them. Then get into small groups and share your opinion.

Step 4 Of the different ideas you heard in this activity, which one(s) are you the most interested in ? Why?

104

Quick Quiz Answer: d

Action Worksheet

This section consists of a full-page worksheet to be used together with the "Action" section in each chapter. This worksheet enables the students to compile and keep their own portfolios as a record of what they have learned and how it has affected their behavior.

Table of Contents

PROLOGUE

Beginning the Journey

We are determined to take the bold and transformative steps which are urgently needed to shift the world onto a sustainable and resilient path. As we embark on this collective journey, we pledge that no one will be left behind.

UN (2015) Transforming Our World: The 2030 Agenda for Sustainable Development

Chapter 1 Global Perspectives

To be able to tackle global issues effectively, it is not enough for us to merely have a passing knowledge about what the issues are. Rather, we are required to develop global perspectives that enable us to understand what the issues entail and how they relate to our daily lives. In this first section, we will learn about global perspectives as a basis for transforming the world through our day-to-day actions.

Sweet Peas
Meaning: Departure

Chapter 1

Global Perspectives

Introduction

1. Have you ever heard of "SDGs"? What do you think the three initials stand for?

2. The SDGs are a set of seventeen goals which, if achieved, will make the world a better place. If you could change anything to make the world a better place, what would you change? Why?

Vocabulary List

Match the words with the definitions below. Look up the definition and review the synonyms.

No.	Word	Definition	Definition in my language	Synonyms
1	**universal (adj.)**	d	世界中の、普遍的な	global, broad
2	**diverse (adj.)**			differing, not alike
3	**represent (v.)**			equal, mean
4	**perspective (n.)**			opinion, viewpoint
5	**characteristic (n.)**			personality, style
6	**interconnected (adj.)**			linked, similar
7	**passive (adj.)**			quiet, uninvolved
8	**solution (n.)**			result, answer
9	**discrimination (n.)**			hate, unfairness
10	**alternative (adj.)**			different, (an) other

Key: n. = noun, v. = verb, adj. = adjective, adv. = adverb

Definitions

a. the position from which you think about something or view something
b. describing a choice, plan, or method that differs from that previously decided upon
c. the answer to a question or problem
d. relating to everyone in the world or to everyone in a particular group
e. not acting to change a situation; allowing others to be in control
f. including many different types; varied
g. a feature that makes one person or thing different from others
h. treating a particular type of person or group of people differently, often in a worse way
i. having different parts connected to or related to each other
j. to be the equivalent of something or to symbolize something

Key words for understanding the SDGs

- Sustainability = the quality of being able to be maintained over time
- Development = improvement toward a better society in which everyone can use their abilities and live happily

Reading Preview

Scan the Reading Passage and choose the paragraph number (1–5) that matches the pictures below.

(A) Paragraph No. _______

(B) Paragraph No. _______

(C) Paragraph No. _______

(D) Paragraph No. _______

(E) Paragraph No. _______

Reading Passage

Common Goals for the Future

DL 2

[1] The Sustainable Development Goals (SDGs) are a set of **universal** goals to make a better world. All of the member states at the 2015 United Nations General Assembly agreed upon them. The SDGs clarified the global challenges that both developed and developing countries need to tackle in three areas: the environment, society, and the economy. Importantly, these goals were not simply created by government organizations but also by a **diverse** range of groups including companies, NPOs, minorities, and young people. The SDGs **represent** everyone and are based on the collective voices of people from around the world.

[2] The SDGs aim to change our future and reflect a vision of our world in 2030. They are made up of seventeen goals and 169 targets for achieving them. Each goal focuses on a different important issue such as climate change or poverty. It may seem impossible to tackle so many different problems on such a large scale. However, if we view the SDGs from "global **perspectives**," we can see that they all share certain **characteristics**. Let's take a look at three key perspectives and how they relate to the SDGs.

[3] The first perspective is *making connections*. All of the goals outlined in the SDGs are **interconnected** with each other. This means that rather than trying to tackle all seventeen goals at the same time, we can start with one and use it as a gateway for dealing with other issues. The problems facing our world are very complex, so we first need to understand how they are related to each other on a global scale. We also need to be aware of how they connect

with our daily lives. In other words, in order to solve the world's problems, we cannot think of ourselves as **passive** outsiders. Instead, we should take daily steps toward a **solution**.

[4] The second perspective is *recognizing differences*. The SDGs aim for a world without **discrimination** in which "no one is left behind." They take a holistic approach in which everyone from you and me to different vulnerable groups, animals, and even the environment is included. To achieve this, we should try to accept diversity and recognize that there is more than one perspective on any single issue. There is no single "right answer" to any of the problems identified by the SDGs. Different possible answers will be created as we tackle the world's biggest problems together.

[5] The final perspective is *looking to the future*. According to the SDGs, just learning about the issues is not enough. To change the world, we need to reflect on our own individual lifestyles and values. The problems we are facing are difficult to overcome, so people from different backgrounds must come together to work toward their common goals. The future is not set in stone. There are many possible **alternative** futures depending on the actions we take today. Even if we choose to do nothing, it will still affect our common future.

Check Your Understanding

Answer the following questions about the Reading Passage.

1. What are the three global perspectives that are shared by all of the SDGs?

2. Why isn't our future "set in stone"?

3. According to the passage, which of the following statements is **NOT** true about the SDGs?
   a. The SDGs are a set of universal goals agreed upon by both developing and developed countries.
   b. The SDGs are all interconnected with each other.
   c. The SDGs contain seventeen goals and 169 targets based on a vision of how the world might appear in 2030.
   d. The SDGs were mostly created by government organizations.

4. What does taking a "holistic approach" mean for solving the world's problems?
   a. It means that there is only one perspective for each issue.
   b. It means that we should consider everyone, including animals and the environment.
   c. It means that we should try to tackle all seventeen goals at the same time.
   d. It means that we should become passive outsiders in order to find new solutions.

Vocabulary Review

Fill in the blanks with the words from the box below. Change the form of the words if necessary.

universal	**diverse**	**represent**	**perspective**	**characteristic**
interconnected	**passive**	**solution**	**discrimination**	**alternative**

1. One aim of the SDGs is for a world without ________________ where everyone is treated equally.
2. To many people, cherry blossom trees ________________ the beauty of Japan.
3. Communicative ability is one of the most important ________________ that companies look for in new employees.
4. Hitomi's study abroad experience in India has given her a unique ________________ on Indian culture.
5. The bridge was closed this morning, so Bill had to use an ________________ route to get to work.
6. Music is thought of as a ________________ language because everyone can appreciate it.
7. We can't be ________________ in our action against climate change. All of us need to actively take steps to overcome it.

Listening Comprehension

Listen to two students having a conversation on the train. Use the words in the box below to complete the summary of the conversation.

DL 3

While on her way to school, Sally sees a 1.________________ about the SDGs in the train. She recently learned about the SDGs in her 2.________________ class, so she tells James about them. Sally explains that they include broad goals such as making 3.________________ available to everyone and promoting equality. Importantly, they encourage people to make 4.________________ in their daily lives. Sally refers to coffee shops that no longer use 5.________________ as an example. They decide to 6.________________ some of the other goals before class.

Global Studies	**large changes**	**clean water**
plastic cups	**poster**	**plastic straws**
small changes	**look up**	**Environmental Studies**

Sustainable Development Goals

In this section of each chapter, you will be introduced to SDGs relating to the chapter's content. In addition, this section will ask you to *make connections*, *recognize differences*, and *look to the future* from global perspectives.

Making Connections

The pictures below show some global issues. How do they make the world unsustainable? Choose one and write a few sentences to explain your thoughts. Then discuss them with a partner.

Global Warming

Nuclear Weapons

Plastic Waste

My reaction

Action **Getting to Know the SDGs**

In this activity, you will become familiar with the SDGs. Go to page 104 for details.

SDGs Quick Quiz

Can you guess the answer to the following question? Test your knowledge.

The Doomsday Clock shows how close human life is to ending at midnight. According to the Doomsday Clock, how much time is left until the end of the world?

a. 3 hours to midnight
b. 1 hour to midnight
c. 10 minutes to midnight
d. 100 seconds to midnight

Check your answer on page 104.

PART ONE

The Environment

You don't know how to fix the holes in our ozone layer.
You don't know how to bring salmon back up a dead stream.
You don't know how to bring back an animal now extinct.
And you can't bring back forests that once grew where there is now a desert.
If you don't know how to fix it, please stop breaking it!

Severn Cullis-Suzuki speaking at the Earth Summit in Rio de Janeiro, 1992

Chapter 2 Climate Change
Chapter 3 Water
Chapter 4 Clean Energy

Our way of living has a great impact on the global environment.
Conversely, the environment has a great influence on our daily lives.
In this section, we will look at the nature of the relationship between human life and the environment through the exploration of three themes: climate change, water, and clean energy.

Magnolias
Meaning: Love of Nature

Chapter 2

Climate Change

Introduction

1. You've probably heard of "global warming." What is one cause of global warming?

2. Have you ever experienced harsh weather such as unusually high temperatures in summer or strong typhoons? Take a moment to think about one of your experiences and share it with a partner.

Vocabulary List

Match the words with the definitions below. Look up the definition and review the synonyms.

No.	Word	Definition	Definition in my language	Synonyms
1	**climate (n.)**	b	気候	temperature, weather
2	**tragedy (n.)**			disaster, hardship
3	**headline (n.)**			story, title
4	**starvation (n)**			famine, malnutrition
5	**irreversible (adj.)**			permanent, unchangeable
6	**devastating (adj.)**			damaging, destructive
7	**emission (n.)**			discharge, outpouring
8	**abolish (v.)**			cancel, put an end to
9	**mock (v.)**			insult, tease
10	**reluctant (adj.)**			cautious, hesitant

Key: n. = noun, v. = verb, adj. = adjective, adv. = adverb

Definitions

a. describing something that cannot go back to how it was before
b. the weather conditions usually experienced by a particular geographic region
c. to officially end something, especially a law or system
d. an event or situation that is very sad and often involves death
e. to laugh at someone or something in an unkind way
f. the state of not having enough food, often causing sickness or death
g. causing a lot of damage or destruction
h. not wanting to do something
i. the title of a news article; the main story in a newspaper or on a news website
j. something (such as gas, heat, radiation, or light) sent out into the air, often as a waste product

Vocabulary Tip

il- / ir- / im- / in- are all prefixes meaning **"not"**

Which prefix you should use depends on the first letter of the word it will be attached to.

First letter	Prefix	Examples
L	il-	illegal, illiterate
R	ir-	irreversible, irresponsible
P, M, B	im-	impolite, immature, imbalanced
All others	in-	inexpensive, independent, insane

Reading Preview

Scan the Reading Passage and choose the paragraph number (1–5) that matches the pictures below.

(A) Paragraph No. ______

(B) Paragraph No. ______

(C) Paragraph No. ______

Climate
Crisis

(D) Paragraph No. ______

(E) Paragraph No. ______

Reading Passage

Running Out of Time

DL 4

[1] Recently, we often hear phrases like "the hottest weather in fifty years" or "the heaviest rainfall in a century" on the news. It seems that almost every year, Japan is hit with record-setting rainfall, often resulting in great damage. ***Climate change*** is mainly caused by global warming and is a major reason for extreme weather events such as heatwaves, floods, typhoons, and droughts. In fact, climate change has become such a serious problem that it is being referred to as the "climate crisis."

[2] The impact of climate change on the world is wide-ranging. **Tragedies** like the Australian bushfires that killed nearly a billion animals make **headlines**, but extreme weather conditions are endangering wildlife everywhere. According to the IUCN Red List, more than 1,750 species are endangered because of global warming. Of course, climate change affects humans, too. Extreme weather can ruin crops, destroying small farming communities and leaving people without food. In developing countries, food and water shortages can cause **starvation**, the spread of disease, and regional conflicts.

[3] We must act quickly to avoid the **irreversible** effects of global warming. Scientists predict that the Earth will heat up by around 4 degrees Celsius by 2100. This would be **devastating** to humans, animals, and the environment. In response, developed and developing countries from around the world came together in 2015 to draw up the Paris Agreement. The

agreement aims to limit the rise in temperature to 2 degrees Celsius with 1.5 degrees Celsius as an ideal goal. This will be extremely difficult to achieve, even if the entire world works together. In order to do this, scientists estimate that global greenhouse gas **emissions** must be reduced to almost zero by 2050.

[4] To fulfill its commitments to the Paris Agreement, Japan will have to make significant changes. In fact, Japan is the fifth highest CO_2 emitting country in the world. Nearly 40 percent of Japan's greenhouse gas emissions are from power plants, half of which are coal-powered. Burning coal releases a lot of CO_2, so it must be internationally **abolished** to meet the goals set by the Paris Agreement. Despite this, Japan has announced that it will continue to use coal power and has even developed new coal plants. Shamefully, Japan has been awarded a **mocking** "Fossil" award for being **reluctant** to tackle global warming.

[5] You may be thinking, "If entire countries won't change their ways, what good can my individual actions do?" Fortunately, there is a lot we can do. About 20 percent of Japan's CO_2 emissions come from people's homes, so by making efforts to save electricity, we can make a real difference. We can also find like-minded people and work together to address climate change. In 2018, a young girl with a handmade sign sat down in front of Sweden's parliament building. Since then, her small protest has become the largest social climate movement ever. When we work together, even the smallest actions can lead to great things.

Check Your Understanding

Answer the following questions about the Reading Passage.

1. What can happen as a result of water shortages in developing countries?

2. What is the goal of the Paris Agreement?

3. According to the passage, which of the following statements is true of Japan?
   a. There are only four other countries in the world that produce more CO_2 than Japan.
   b. Japan won an award for fulfilling its commitments to the Paris Agreement.
   c. Japan has stopped making coal-burning power plants.
   d. Nearly 40 percent of Japan's greenhouse gas emissions come from people's homes.

4. Why do scientists say that global greenhouse gas emissions must be reduced to almost zero in the next thirty years?
   a. To heat up the Earth by 4 degrees Celsius
   b. To meet the temperature goal set by the Paris Agreement
   c. To prevent protests and social movements
   d. To save electricity

Vocabulary Review

Fill in the blanks with the words from the box below. Change the form of the words if necessary.

climate	tragedy	headline	starvation	irreversible
devastating	emission	abolish	mock	reluctant

1. The earthquake and tsunami in Tohoku, Japan was a ____________________ that many communities are still recovering from.
2. It's not nice to ____________________ people when they make mistakes. After all, we all make mistakes sometimes.
3. Climate change has caused ____________________ damage to our environment that can never be completely fixed.
4. The practice of burning coal releases a lot of CO_2 into the air, so it must be ____________________ if we want to stop global warming.
5. The local news story became an international ____________________ when it was featured on a popular news website.
6. The student was ____________________ to go to school because he had not studied for his exam.
7. Sadly, millions of people die every year from ____________________ because they do not have access to food.

Listening Comprehension

Listen to two students having a conversation at school. Use the words in the box below to complete the summary of the conversation.

DL 5

Sally will go to Tokyo 1.________________________. She plans to 2.________________________ a demonstration about climate change. The demonstration is part of a worldwide social movement called "Fridays for 3.________________________." It was started by 4.________________________ and encourages 5.________________________ to help the environment. James thinks the event sounds 6.________________________, so he decides to join Sally.

scientists	this weekend	young people
a Swedish girl	interesting	next week
the Planet	check out	Future

13 CLIMATE ACTION

SDG 13: Climate Action

The aim of SDG 13 is to take urgent action against climate change and to reduce its environmental impact. Climate change has been directly linked to our daily lifestyle habits. Everyone, therefore, has a part to play in tackling this problem.

Looking to the Future

The pictures below show things that will possibly happen if the Earth's temperature rises by 4 degrees Celsius. Think about how these changes may affect future generations. Write a few sentences to explain your thoughts and discuss them with a partner.

Extreme Weather

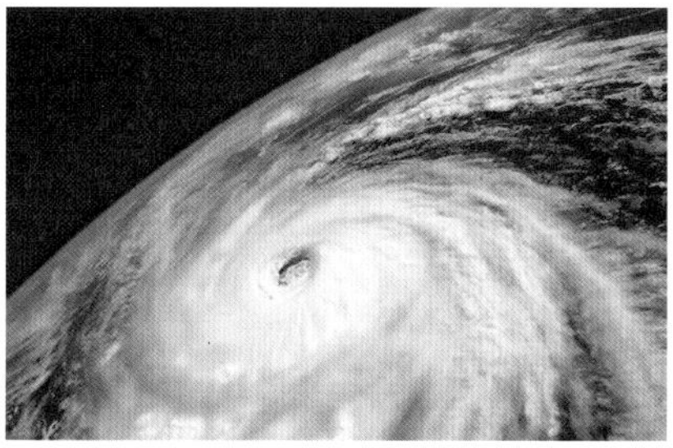

- Typhoons bigger than ever before
- More frequent flooding

Ocean Life

- 99% of coral reefs to die
- 25% reduction in catchable fish

Global Economy

- 30% less economic production
- Worldwide food shortages

My reaction

Action What Can We Do to Tackle Climate Change?

In this activity, you will brainstorm the different everyday actions we can take to help prevent climate change. Go to page 105 for details.

SDGs Quick Quiz

Can you guess the answer to the following SDGs-related question? Test your knowledge.

What percentage of animal species may disappear by 2070 as a result of climate change?

a. 10 percent b. 20 percent c. 30 percent d. 50 percent

Check your answer on page 105.

Chapter 3

Water

Introduction

1. Do you have a river or a lake near your home? Would you drink from it if the water stopped running at your home?

2. What do you think the girls are doing in the photographs below? Share your thoughts with a partner.

Vocabulary List

Match the words with the definitions below. Look up the definition and review the synonyms.

No.	Word	Definition	Definition in my language	Synonyms
1	**valuable (adj.)**	g	高価な、貴重な	expensive
2	**resource (n.)**			supply, material
3	**scarcity (n.)**			lack, shortage
4	**effective (adj.)**			useful, helpful
5	**estimate (v.)**			guess, approximate
6	**burden (n.)**			load, duty
7	**contribute (v.)**			partially cause, lead to
8	**crisis (n.)**			emergency, disaster
9	**despite (prep.)**			in spite of, regardless of
10	**conscious (adj.)**			aware, alert

Key: n. = noun, v. = verb, adj. = adjective, adv. = adverb, prep. = preposition

Definitions

a. a situation in which someone or something has a very serious problem
b. something difficult or worrying that you have to deal with
c. used to say something happened or is true, although it seems unlikely
d. a situation in which there is not enough of something
e. successful or having the result that you want
f. to be one of the causes of something that happens
g. worth a lot of money; very useful
h. knowing that something is present or is happening
i. to make a reasonable guess
j. something that is useful and available for use

Study Tip

Learn new words by drawing pictures to connect the words with their meanings. Give it a try!

Reading Preview

Scan the Reading Passage and choose the paragraph number (1–5) that matches the pictures below.

(A) Paragraph No. _______

(B) Paragraph No. _______

(C) Paragraph No. _______

(D) Paragraph No. _______

(E) Paragraph No. _______

Reading Passage

The Value of a Single Drop

DL 6

[1] Have you ever thought about just how **valuable** drinking water is? Even though Earth is sometimes called "the water planet," only around 0.01 percent of Earth's water can be accessed and used by humans. In other words, if all of the water on Earth were in a five hundred milliliter bottle, the amount that humans would actually be able to use for drinking and agriculture would be less than a single drop. Fresh water is necessary for human life, but, currently, there is not enough for everyone. Water is, therefore, one of the most important natural **resources** of our time.

[2] Humans everywhere depend on water, and as the world's population grows, so does its impact on the environment. Pumping too much water from the ground, for example, can cause wells and rivers to run dry. The Aral Sea, which was once the fourth largest lake in the world, has almost disappeared as a result of water from the rivers that feed it being taken for irrigation. Furthermore, even some of the world's largest rivers, such as the Nile and the Indus, are in danger of drying up.

[3] A lack of water—called *water* ***scarcity***—affects people all over the world. Many developing countries do not have **effective** systems for accessing and cleaning water. People without ready access to water often have to travel very far from their homes every day just to collect it. It is **estimated** that about one-third of the population in Sub-Saharan Africa must

travel at least thirty minutes to the closest water source, often several times a day. This **burden** falls mainly on women and girls. As a result, many women cannot do any other work, and many young girls cannot attend school. Children are also usually the first to get sick or die from drinking dirty water.

[4] People in developed countries like Japan may feel that this problem does not relate to them, but this is not the case. Developed countries **contribute** to this problem in a major way through their use of *virtual water*. Virtual water refers to the total amount of water used to make and transport food and products like clothing and electronics. For example, when considering the amount of water it takes to raise, prepare, and transport beef, a single hamburger uses about 2,400 liters! Japan is the second largest virtual water importer in the world and, as such, shares responsibility for the Earth's water **crisis**.

[5] **Despite** the development of new technologies enabling us to extract more water from the environment (such as desalination, which enables us to remove salt from seawater), there is still no simple solution to the water scarcity problem. However, by becoming more **conscious** of our daily habits, we can reduce our water use by thousands of liters a year. This will be of benefit to both our local environments and the global environment, allowing more people around the world to enjoy fresh, clean water.

Check Your Understanding

Answer the following questions about the Reading Passage.

1. Why is clean water "one of the most important natural resources of our time"?

2. What is *virtual water*?

3. According to the passage, why are many large rivers and lakes in danger of becoming dry?
   a. Large animal populations in places like Africa drink too much water.
   b. Too much water is used to transport goods and products to other countries.
   c. Too much water is pumped from the ground or taken from rivers to be used for irrigation.
   d. People are drinking too much water with their hamburgers.

4. How does water scarcity affect children in developing countries? *(You can circle more than one correct answer.)*
   a. Many children in developing countries have to travel long distances every day to collect water.
   b. Children are often the first to become sick from drinking unclean water.
   c. Many children spend so much time carrying water that they cannot attend school.
   d. Children must sell water in order to pay for an education.

Vocabulary Review

Fill in the blanks with the words from the box below. Change the form of the words if necessary.

valuable	**resource**	**scarcity**	**effective**	**estimate**
burden	**contribute**	**crisis**	**despite**	**conscious**

1. ____________________ the heavy snowfall, the buses are still running.
2. It's important to protect natural ____________________ such as water and oil.
3. Exercising for thirty minutes every day is an ____________________ way to stay healthy.
4. Scientists ____________________ that the average person in Japan uses 286 liters of water a day.
5. Brandon worried that his long working hours were a ____________________ on his family.
6. My city recently started a poster campaign to make people more ____________________ of wasteful water habits.
7. It's a good idea to keep a supply of food and water at home in case of a ____________________ such an earthquake.

Listening Comprehension

Listen to two students having a conversation in the school cafeteria. Use the words in the box below to complete the summary of the conversation.

DL 7

James wasn't going to 1.____________________ his soup because he was full, so he 2.____________________ it to Sally. James thinks that there is nothing wrong with 3.____________________ his unfinished food. Sally explains that if a person throws away a 200 milliliter bowl of 4.____________________, it must be mixed with around 1,500 liters of water before the 5.____________________ is good enough for fish to be able to live in it. James decides to be more 6.____________________ in the future.

miso soup	**corn soup**	**water quality**	**eating**	**finish**
hungry	**offered**	**careful**	**throwing away**	

SDG 6: Clean Water and Sanitation

The aim of SDG 6 is to ensure access to clean water and sanitation for everyone. People in some countries do not have access to clean water. This results in the spread of disease and many deaths. Let's think about the connection between clean water and good health.

Making Connections

Think about the pictures below. How do they connect with each other? Write a few sentences to explain your thoughts and discuss them with a partner.

Dirty Drinking Water

No Access to Soap

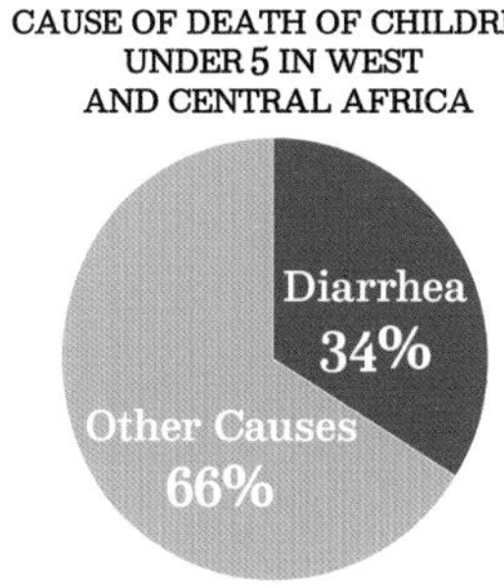

Disease

My reaction

Action Checking Our Water Use

In this activity, you will think about your own use of water and how we can reduce waste. Go to page 106 for details.

SDGs Quick Quiz

Can you guess the answer to the following SDGs-related question? Test your knowledge.

Where does the dirtiest water come from in a house?

a. The toilet b. The kitchen sink c. The bath d. The washing machine

Check your answer on page 106.

Chapter 4

Clean Energy

Introduction

1. What different sources of energy can you think of?

2. If you did not have electric lights in your home, how would it affect your life? What things would you no longer be able to do? Share your answers with a partner.

Vocabulary List

Match the words with the definitions below. Look up the definition and review the synonyms.

No.	Word	Definition	Definition in my language	Synonyms
1	**conflict (n.)**	c	紛争、対立	fighting, war
2	**reliable (adj.)**			trustworthy
3	**enormous (adj.)**			huge, massive
4	**sustainable (adj.)**			continuous
5	**renewable (adj.)**			endless, limitless
6	**abundant (adj.)**			large in number, ample
7	**affordable (adj.)**			cheap, reasonable
8	**debate (v.)**			discuss, argue
9	**minimize (v.)**			lessen, reduce
10	**accordingly (adv.)**			appropriately, properly

Key: n. = noun, v. = verb, adj. = adjective, adv. = adverb

Definitions

a. able to be used and easily replaced without running out
b. able to be trusted or believed
c. fighting between groups or countries
d. able to continue over a period of time
e. more than enough; a lot of
f. in a way that is suitable or right for the situation
g. to make the amount of something as small as possible
h. to try to make a decision about something through discussion
i. extremely large
j. not expensive; can be bought by people who don't have much money

Study Tip

The suffix **"-able"** (sometimes "**-ible**") means **"possible to do**." You can easily turn many verbs into adjectives by using these suffixes.

afford → afford**able**	convert → convert**ible**	enjoy → enjoy**able**
flex → flex**ible**	reduce → reduc**ible**	rely → reli**able**
renew → renew**able**	sustain → sustain**able**	value → valu**able**

Reading Preview

Scan the Reading Passage and choose the paragraph number (1–5) that matches the pictures below.

(A) Paragraph No. ______

(B) Paragraph No. ______

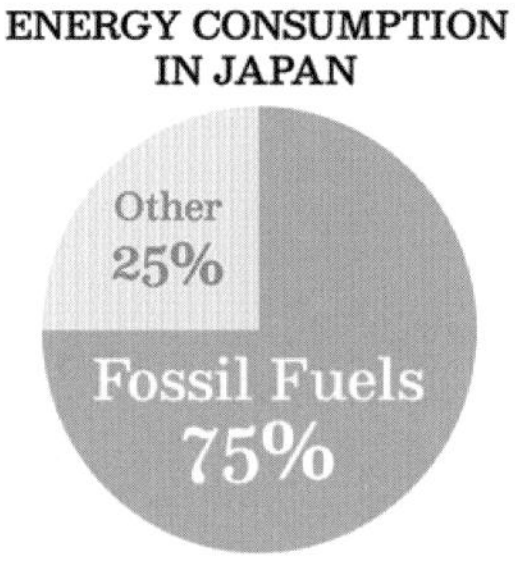

(C) Paragraph No. ______

(D) Paragraph No. ______

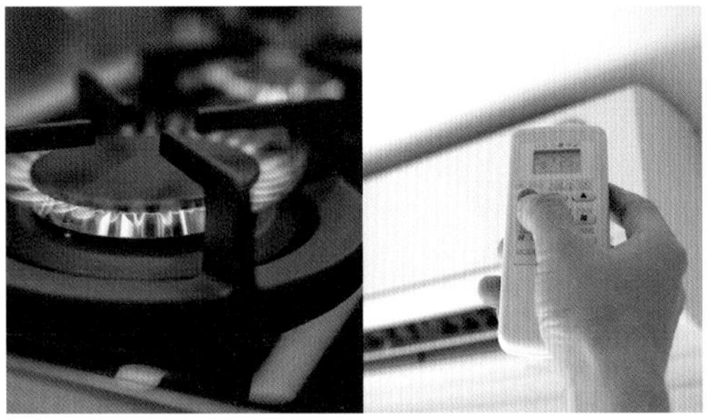

(E) Paragraph No. ______

Reading Passage

Before We Run Out

DL 8

[1] Almost every item we interact with needs energy. But what would happen if the world ran out of energy? You wouldn't be able to use the air conditioning even during the hottest summer, nor would you be able to cook a delicious meal on your stove. As the world's population approaches eight billion, there already isn't enough energy for everyone. In fact, scientists predict that we will run out of our main source of energy—fossil fuels—within this century. Securing energy is so important that it has even been the cause of **conflicts**. Something must change.

[2] It is estimated that over 1.1 billion people in developing countries are living without a **reliable** source of electricity. These people often must burn wood and coal for heating and cooking, leaving them with dirty air and no light after dark. Meanwhile, in developed countries, **enormous** amounts of fossil fuels are burned for people to have comfortable lives, polluting the air and greatly contributing to climate change. For both developed and developing countries, this way of life is not **sustainable**. We must, therefore, seek out alternative energy sources.

[3] "Clean energy," or energy that is **renewable** and does not produce harmful emissions, offers solutions to the energy problems faced by all countries. In developing countries, biomass energy is becoming a reliable energy source because it makes use of **abundant** animal and

plant materials. For instance, solar-biomass stoves that can cleanly heat, cook, and generate electricity are now being produced, offering a renewable and **affordable** energy source to millions. Meanwhile, in developed countries, clean energy sources like wind, solar, and geothermal energy are becoming more common. Clean energy provides 40 percent or more of some European countries' energy requirements.

[4] Japan, on the other hand, is still heavily dependent on fossil fuels, which account for roughly 75 percent of its energy consumption. In addition, coal accounts for roughly 40 percent of Japan's fossil-fuel output, despite emitting more CO_2 than any other fossil fuel. Nuclear energy might offer one possible solution, but its safety is being thoroughly **debated** following the 2011 disaster in Fukushima. No matter how difficult, we must reduce our reliance on fossil fuels and create a new reality with clean energy. It is our collective responsibility to **minimize** harm to the environment and preserve the Earth for future generations.

[5] Recently in Japan, there has been a movement toward creating a "recycling-oriented society." This movement aims to reduce single-use plastics and other types of waste in our daily lives. It also encourages us to think more deeply about the environment and our energy needs, and to adjust our lifestyles **accordingly**. Examples include using public transportation or ridesharing instead of driving, installing solar panels on our homes, and pressuring local governments to create bicycle paths. By being more mindful of our current energy use and our future energy needs, together we can create a clean environment to enjoy for many years to come.

Check Your Understanding

Answer the following questions about the Reading Passage.

1. Why must both developing and developed countries look for different energy sources?

2. What are the benefits of a solar-biomass stove?

3. Which of the following actions represents a "recycling-oriented society"? (*You can circle more than one correct answer.*)
   a. Taking a reusable shopping bag to the store instead of using single-use plastic bags
   b. Driving to work alone every day instead of taking public transportation
   c. Taking a washable water bottle to school instead of buying drinks from a vending machine
   d. Using air conditioning in the summer instead of opening a window

4. According to the passage, which of the following statements is **NOT** true of fossil fuels?
   a. Most of Japan's energy comes from burning fossil fuels.
   b. We cannot use fossil fuels forever because they will eventually run out.
   c. We should continue to use fossil fuels for the sake of future generations.
   d. Burning fossil fuels causes air pollution.

Vocabulary Review

Fill in the blanks with the words from the box below. Change the form of the words if necessary.

conflict	**reliable**	**enormous**	**sustainable**	**renewable**
abundant	**affordable**	**debate**	**minimize**	**accordingly**

1. Many people died as a result of the ________________ between the two countries.
2. That cat is ________________! It must be the biggest cat I've ever seen!
3. The world needs to increase its use of ________________ energy because fossil fuels are running out.
4. There is ________________ sunlight in this area, so the city is planning to build a solar power station.
5. Those apartments look expensive, but they are actually very ________________.
6. It's important to reduce CO_2 emissions as much as possible in order to ________________ damage to the environment.
7. Millions of people worldwide must burn wood and coal for heating and cooking because they don't have a ________________ source of electricity.

Listening Comprehension

Listen to two students having a conversation at school. Use the words in the box below to complete the summary of the conversation.

DL 9

James is in a 1.________________________ because his electricity bill was 2.________________________ than he had expected. He thinks the reason is because his new apartment has an energy-efficient 3.________________________ and air conditioner. His apartment also has LED light bulbs that 4.________________________ turn off when he leaves the room. They are more efficient and last 5.________________________ than regular light bulbs. James plans to thank his 6.________________________.

lower	**apartment manager**	**water heater**
longer	**larger**	**washing machine**
good mood	**automatically**	**bad mood**

SDG 7: Affordable and Clean Energy

The aim of SDG 7 is to provide people with affordable and clean energy. The modern world depends on fossil fuels, which are a major cause of global warming. They are also limited, so their use is unsustainable. Let's think about how we can produce clean energy in the future.

Recognizing Differences

The graphs below show how clean energy is used in the world, in Japan, and in Germany. How does Japan's data compare with the other data sets? How should Japan adapt to clean energy in the future? Write a few sentences to explain your thoughts and discuss them with a partner.

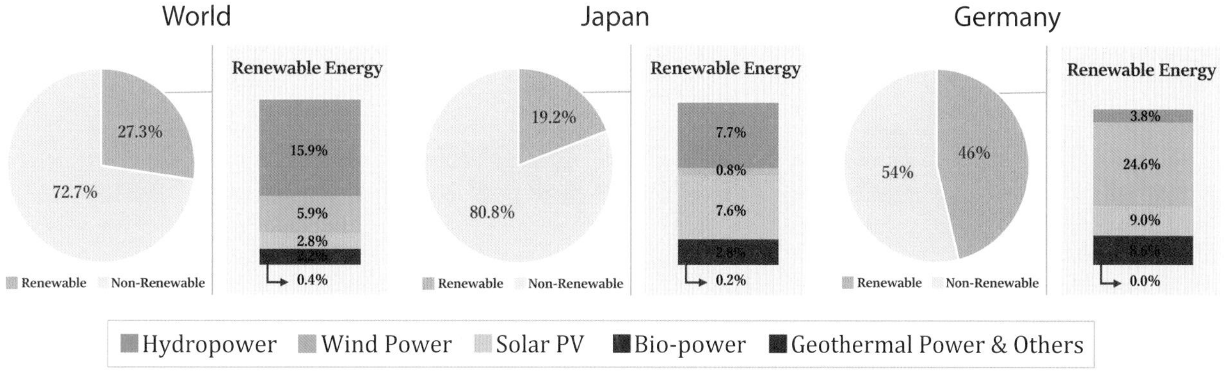

My reaction

Action Imagining the Future of Energy

In this activity, you will think of creative ways we may use renewable energy sources in the future. Go to page 107 for details.

SDGs Quick Quiz

Can you guess the answer to the following SDGs-related question? Test your knowledge.

Which of the renewable energy types below produces the most electricity worldwide?

a. Wind power b. Solar power c. Geothermal power d. Bio-power

Check your answer on page 107.

PART TWO

Development

Some consume the Earth's resources at a rate that would leave little for future generations. Others, many more in number, consume far too little and live with the prospect of hunger, squalor, disease, and early death.

UN (1987) Our Common Future

Chapter 5 Poverty
Chapter 6 Hunger
Chapter 7 Children

A huge economic gap exists between the richer countries and the poorer countries of the world. The problems faced by these two groups might appear to be very different but are in fact interrelated and derived from the same causes. In this section, we will look at how global issues relate to local issues through the exploration of three themes: poverty, hunger, and children.

Daisies
Meanings: Peace, Harmony

Chapter 5

Poverty

Introduction

1. How much money do you need to live a comfortable life? Do you think it's the same amount of money for people in other countries? Why?

2. What do you think are some of the challenges faced by children growing up in poverty? Share your ideas with a partner.

Vocabulary List

Match the words with the definitions below. Look up the definition and review the synonyms.

No.	Word	Definition	Definition in my language	Synonyms
1	**fulfilling (adj.)**	c	充実した	satisfying
2	**absolute (adj.)**			complete, total
3	**vulnerable (adj.)**			unsafe, at risk
4	**factor (n.)**			influence, component
5	**infrastructure (n.)**			base, framework
6	**relative (adj.)**			connected, related
7	**median (adj.)**			middle, center
8	**stimulate (v.)**			support, promote
9	**disadvantage (n)**			downside, difficulty
10	**donate (v.)**			give, contribute

Key: n. = noun, v. = verb, adj. = adjective, adv. = adverb

Definitions

a. one of many things that cause or influence a situation
b. the basic systems and structures that enable an organization or country to function
c. making you feel happy and satisfied
d. able to be easily harmed or hurt
e. something that causes problems or that makes someone or something less likely to succeed
f. being related to or able to be compared with something else in a particular way
g. to encourage something to grow, develop, or become active
h. being the middle number in a set of numbers that have been arranged in order
i. true, constant, and unlimited
j. to give something to a person or organization so as to help them

Reading Preview

Scan the Reading Passage and choose the paragraph number (1–5) that matches the pictures below.

(A) Paragraph No. ________

(B) Paragraph No. ________

(C) Paragraph No. ________

(D) Paragraph No. ________

(E) Paragraph No. ________

Reading Passage

Leaving No One Behind

DL 10

[1] How much money do you need to live? Could you live on only two hundred yen a day? Perhaps you could survive, but you would not be able to afford all of the things you need to live a healthy, **fulfilling** life. *Poverty* is a situation in which a person struggles to afford daily necessities, and, according to the World Bank, it affects nearly half the world's population. It is such a big problem that the first goal of the SDGs is to end poverty.

[2] There are approximately 700 million people around the world currently living in ***absolute** poverty*. This means that they are living on less than 1.9 US dollars a day. These people cannot pay for even the most basic human needs such as water, food, and clothing. Of course, they cannot afford an education, making it difficult for the next generation to escape poverty. Women—especially single mothers—and children are particularly **vulnerable**, and external **factors** such as war and natural disasters only add to the challenge of surviving from day to day.

[3] Why are so many people living in poverty while others enjoy a life of wealth? One of the major reasons is that global trade is unequal and heavily favors developed countries. Developing countries often do not have advanced technology or a skilled workforce. As a result, their industrial output is often limited to low-priced exports such as lumber, mined raw materials, and cheap agricultural products. These countries cannot afford to improve the **infrastructures** necessary to develop their economies. Thus, the economic gap between

developing and developed countries widens as this cycle continues.

[4] Wealthy countries are not free from poverty. Nowadays, about one in seven people in Japan lives in ***relative** poverty*. This means that their annual income is less than half the approximate national **median** income, or less than 1.2 million yen a year. More than half of single-parent households in Japan live in relative poverty. Single parents must not only work but must also do the housework and take care of the children by themselves. As a result, by comparison with other households, their household incomes are relatively low. Furthermore, some children may not have a home environment that **stimulates** their education or may face other **disadvantages**.

[5] In Japan, some community residents, NPOs, and local governments are taking action to reduce the effects of poverty. They have started programs such as the *Kodomo Shokudo* ("Children's Cafeteria"), providing children with free or low-cost meals and other services. Such programs are often staffed by student volunteers who not only feed the children but also spend time with them and help them learn. Foodbanks, where people can **donate** unused food to the needy, are also becoming more common. By only giving a little of our own time and resources, we can make a real difference and help the vulnerable members of our society. We must all do our part to make sure that "no one is left behind."

Check Your Understanding

Answer the following questions about the Reading Passage.

1. What difficulties do people in *absolute poverty* often face?

2. What does it mean to live in *relative poverty* in Japan?

3. According to the passage, which of the following contributes to the economic gap between developing and developed countries?
   a. Global trade is unequal and greatly favors developing countries.
   b. Developing countries do not have skilled workers or advanced technology.
   c. Developing countries do not have access to low-priced lumber, mined raw materials, and agricultural products.
   d. Developed countries do not need infrastructures for their economies.

4. According to the passage, which of the following is **NOT** a feature of the *Kodomo Shokudo* program?
   a. Volunteer opportunities for students
   b. Free or low-priced meals for children
   c. Donating food to foodbanks
   d. Spending time with children and helping them learn

Vocabulary Review

Fill in the blanks with the words from the box below. Change the form of the words if necessary.

fulfilling	**absolute**	**vulnerable**	**factor**	**infrastructure**
relative	**median**	**stimulate**	**disadvantage**	**donate**

1. Teachers should ask questions that ____________________ students' imaginations.
2. Poverty, war, and extreme weather are all ____________________ that contribute to the world's hunger problem.
3. Volunteers who work with children usually say that the experience is very ____________________.
4. Most cities have organizations to which people can ____________________ unused food and clothing.
5. The city doesn't have enough money to maintain its ____________________, so many of the roads are in poor condition.
6. A common ____________________ for the children of working parents is that their parents often cannot spend much time with them after school.
7. Small children are ____________________, so they need our help and protection.

Listening Comprehension

Listen to two students having a conversation at school. Use the words in the box below to complete the summary of the conversation.

DL 11

James can't go to 1.____________________ with Sally because he is going to do some volunteer work. He works at *Kodomo Shokudo*, which offers 2.____________________ to the children of low-income families. It's also a place where children can 3.____________________ after class. James helps the children with their 4.____________________ because many of their parents 5.____________________ until late at night and so cannot tutor them. Sally says that she is also 6.____________________ volunteering.

busy with	**a movie**	**money**
a meal service	**spend time**	**the mall**
interested in	**work**	**homework**

SDG 1: No Poverty

The aim of SDG 1 is to end poverty *everywhere*. Poverty is deeply connected to all kinds of other problems. Without enough money, you can't have access to good health care nor can you go to school. Let's think about how poverty connects with other problems.

Making Connections

The pictures below show some of the causes of poverty. Choose one and write a few sentences to explain how it causes poverty. Then discuss your ideas with a partner.

War

Floods

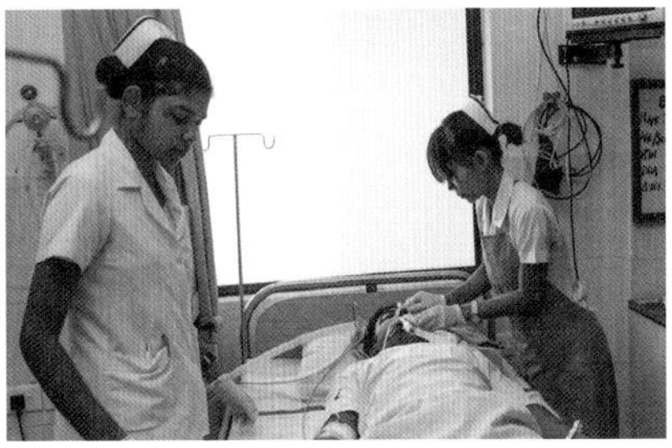

Disease

My reaction

Action World Food Distribution

In this activity, you will learn more about the complex relationship between food supply and different populations. Go to page 108 for details.

SDGs Quick Quiz

Can you guess the answer to the following SDGs-related question? Test your knowledge.

In terms of relative poverty, what is Japan's global ranking out of 40 countries, according to a recent survey by OECD?

a. 5th place b. 14th place c. 21st Place d. 37th place

Check your answer on page 108.

Chapter 6

Hunger

Introduction

1. What's the longest you have ever gone without eating? How did you feel at the time?

2. What do you think convenience stores and supermarkets do with the food that they cannot sell? Share your thoughts with a partner.

Vocabulary List

Match the words with the definitions below. Look up the definition and review the synonyms.

No.	Word	Definition	Definition in my language	Synonyms
1	**nutrition (n.)**	f	栄養、栄養摂取	diet, food
2	**suffer (v.)**			endure
3	**distribute (v.)**			give out, pass out
4	**consume (v)**			eat, take in
5	**livestock (n.)**			farm animals
6	**conditions (n.)**			situation, environment
7	**stable (adj.)**			unmoving, steady
8	**profitable (adj.)**			beneficial, money-making
9	**inefficiently (adv.)**			ineffectively, wastefully
10	**seasonal (adj.)**			occasional, regularly occurring

Key: n. = noun, v. = verb, adj. = adjective, adv. = adverb

Definitions

a. using too much time, money, or energy when performing a task
b. to eat or drink something
c. gaining money or having a beneficial outcome
d. animals that are commonly kept on farms, such as cattle or sheep
e. the factors affecting the situation in which people live and work
f. the beneficial aspects of the food and drink we take into our bodies
g. to share things among a group of people, especially in a planned way
h. firmly fixed; not likely to move or change
i. to experience pain or some other difficult situation
j. happening or existing at a particular time of year

Reading Preview

Scan the Reading Passage and choose the paragraph number (1–5) that matches the pictures below.

(A) Paragraph No. _______

(B) Paragraph No. _______

(C) Paragraph No. _______

(D) Paragraph No. _______

(E) Paragraph No. _______

Reading Passage

Is There Enough Food for Everyone?

DL 12

[1] It's rare for most people in developed countries to miss a meal. However, for much of the world (about one in nine people), not having enough to eat is a daily reality. Hunger is more than just an uncomfortable feeling—it is a matter of life and death. Sadly, about six million children die every year from hunger and poor **nutrition**. However, this is not the result of a lack of food. On the contrary, about 2.6 billion tons of grain products are produced annually, enough to feed approximately double the world's population. So why are so many people **suffering** from hunger?

[2] The biggest reason is that food is unevenly **distributed**. Much of the grain produced around the world isn't directly being **consumed** by humans. Instead, it is being used to feed **livestock**, such as cattle and pigs. Producing one kilogram of beef, for example, requires about eleven kilograms of grain. Much of the world's grain supply is being purchased by developed countries to meet local demand for meat. This causes the international price of grain to go up and makes it difficult for people in poorer countries to buy grain for themselves.

[3] Hunger is also a result of the poor living and working **conditions** found in many developing countries. Poverty, economic slowdown, war, and extreme weather are among the factors contributing to hunger. About 70 percent of people suffering from hunger live in rural areas where these factors make it difficult not only to produce food but also to earn a **stable**

income. Often, these vulnerable people cannot afford food produced in their own countries, as it is more **profitable** for the food producers to sell it to richer countries.

[4] Japan also plays an important role in this problem, as about 60 percent of Japan's total food-calorie consumption comes from imported food. However, much of this food is wasted or used **inefficiently**, with an estimated six million-plus tons of food being thrown away every year. This includes everything from unsold rice balls at the convenience store to produce at the supermarket thrown out for having blemishes. In addition, you may be surprised to learn that while Japan is the world's biggest importer of corn, about three-quarters of it is used only for feeding livestock. Just imagine how many hungry people this food could feed!

[5] Hunger is a complex problem, but there are things we can do to help solve it. For one, if we buy locally produced and **seasonal** foods, Japan's food self-sufficiency will increase. As a result, people in developing countries will be able to buy their locally produced food at affordable prices. Another idea is to reduce the amount of food we waste. One way to do this is to use all of our food before it expires. We can also donate to the foodbanks that distribute food to people in need. By taking these actions, we will help to create a world in which no one has to go to sleep hungry.

Check Your Understanding

Answer the following questions about the Reading Passage.

1. Why do richer countries purchase so much grain?

2. What are two things people in developed countries can do to help solve the global hunger problem?

3. According to the passage, which of the following statements is **NOT** an example of how food is used inefficiently in Japan?
   a. Many people buy locally produced foods.
   b. Most imported corn is used to feed animals.
   c. Convenience stores throw away unsold food, such as rice balls.
   d. Supermarkets throw away food that does not look attractive.

4. According to the passage, which of the following statements is a reason why many people in developing countries cannot get enough food?
   a. There isn't enough food produced in the world to feed everyone.
   b. Since most food is produced in rural areas, people living in cities cannot access it.
   c. Developed countries do not import enough food from developing countries.
   d. Conditions such as poverty and war can make it difficult for people to purchase or access food.

Vocabulary Review

Fill in the blanks with the words from the box below. Change the form of the words if necessary.

nutrition	**suffer**	**distribute**	**consume**	**livestock**
conditions	**stable**	**profitable**	**inefficiently**	**seasonal**

1. Many farmers in developing countries do not have a ____________________ income because the amount of produce they can sell depends on variable factors like the weather.
2. My favorite ____________________ drink is gingerbread latte. It's too bad I can only buy it in the winter.
3. After the earthquake, the government ____________________ supplies such as canned food and toilet paper.
4. ____________________, such as pigs and cattle, eat many times their own weight in grains and other foods.
5. It is often more ____________________ for countries to sell the food they produce to other countries rather than locally to their own citizens.
6. Most people need to ____________________ around 2,000 kilocalories a day to stay healthy.
7. Children in developing countries are more likely to suffer from a lack of ____________________.

Listening Comprehension

Listen to two students having a conversation at school. Use the words in the box below to complete the summary of the conversation.

DL 13

Sally works at a convenience store where food that can't be sold is 1.________________________. This is because it is 2.________________________ to sell it after its expiration date. Stores lose 3.________________________ throwing away unsold food than they do when trying to sell it at a 4.________________________ price. Sally mentions that the Japanese National Diet passed a bill to 5.________________________ food loss reduction. She hopes it will encourage companies to be conscious of wasteful 6.________________________.

more money	**discounted**	**habits**
promote	**thrown away**	**less money**
expensive	**risky**	**safe**

SDG 2: Zero Hunger

The aim of SDG 2 is to end hunger. Many people in poorer countries cannot get enough food to live. Meanwhile, many people in richer countries eat far too much food and throw away large amounts. Let's think about what we can do to end world hunger.

Recognizing Differences

The pictures below show two dietary situations in two countries. First, think about the differences between the pictures. Then think about how they relate to each other. Write a few sentences to explain your thoughts and discuss them with a partner.

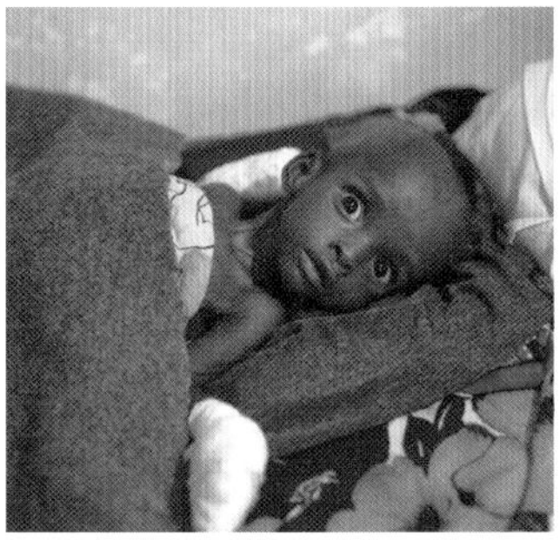
Malnutrition

UN Food Aid

Overeating

Food Waste

My reaction

Action Reducing Our Food Waste

In this activity, you will investigate how much food you waste in the course of a typical week and think about how you can reduce food waste. Go to page 109 for details.

SDGs Quick Quiz

Can you guess the answers to the following SDGs-related questions? Test your knowledge.

About how many people in the world are overweight? How many are obese? Circle two answers below (one for each question).

a. One in three people
b. One in five people
c. One in eight people
d. One in twelve people

Check your answers on page 109.

Chapter 7

Children

Introduction

1. What words and images come to your mind when you hear the words "child labor"?

2. In Japan, some children are raised speaking a language other than Japanese at home. What are some of the difficulties they may face when they start school? Share your answers with a partner.

Vocabulary List

Match the words with the definitions below. Look up the definition and review the synonyms.

No.	Word	Definition	Definition in my language	Synonyms
1	**survey (n.)**	e	調査、検査	investigation, study
2	**struggle (v.)**			try hard, battle
3	**slavery (n)**			captivity, enslavement
4	**recruit (v.)**			enroll, sign up
5	**abuse (v.)**			harm, damage
6	**be engaged (v.)**			be involved, be employed
7	**literacy (n.)**			education, knowledge
8	**primary (adj.)**			elementary, main
9	**immigrant (n.)**			foreigner, newcomer
10	**beneficial (adj.)**			helpful, advantageous

Key: n. = noun, v. = verb, adj. = adjective, adv. = adverb

Definitions

a. to treat someone cruelly
b. the ability to read and write
c. the condition in which someone is owned by someone else and is forced to work
d. to experience difficulty and make a great effort in order to do something
e. an examination of people's opinions or behavior made through the asking of questions
f. to be employed or involved in something, especially work
g. a person who has entered a foreign country in order to live there
h. to persuade someone to join a company or organization, especially the army
i. helpful, useful, or good
j. the first and most essential; used to describe education for young children

Reading Preview

Scan the Reading Passage and choose the paragraph number (1–5) that matches the pictures below.

(A) Paragraph No. ______ (B) Paragraph No. ______ (C) Paragraph No. ______

(D) Paragraph No. ______ (E) Paragraph No. ______

Reading Passage

The World's Forgotten Children

DL 14

[1] Do you like going to school? In a recent **survey** of Japanese high school and junior high school students, about half of the students responded that they "didn't think school is useful" or that they "wouldn't attend if it wasn't required." However, there are hundreds of millions of children around the world who cannot go to school despite wanting to. Without an education, these children are not only more likely to **struggle** socially and economically when they get older but are also statistically more likely to die of preventable diseases.

[2] Poverty is the biggest reason why many children cannot go to school. Families in poorer countries tend to have more children, and these children are often too busy helping their families survive to attend school. Such children spend their daytime hours doing things like helping out with the farm, carrying water, or looking after younger siblings. Some are sold into **slavery** by parents who cannot repay borrowed money. Others who have lost their parents to illness or war become street children or are **recruited** as child soldiers.

[3] Child labor is a key issue relating to education worldwide. It refers to any work that prevents children from getting a basic education, or that is either harmful or dangerous. Children performing that type of labor may work long hours in factories with dirty air, or on farms with dangerous chemicals and no protective gear. In its worst form, child labor takes the shape of forced labor, human trafficking, prostitution, and other scenarios in which the children involved are physically, mentally, or sexually **abused**. Shockingly, about one in ten children

worldwide cannot get a basic education because of work, and one in twenty **is engaged** in the harmful or dangerous scenarios mentioned above.

[4] Even in Japan, where, according to the government, rates for **literacy** and enrollment in **primary** school stand at nearly 100 percent, there are many children who must overcome significant obstacles to getting an education. These include the roughly two million children who are **immigrants** or the children of immigrants. These children may struggle with the Japanese education system for a variety of reasons. Some of them might not be able to understand Japanese well and so might struggle with things such as doing assignments, communicating with their teachers, and making friends. While some of these students receive support from their schools, many go without help and remain at a disadvantage for their entire academic careers.

[5] The level of support varies depending on the local government, with the most supportive starting special programs to help the struggling children catch up. There are also NPOs and other organizations dedicated to helping disadvantaged children. Student volunteer groups have become more common as well, with the volunteers providing free language and learning support. Programs like this are not just **beneficial** to the children; those who volunteer usually report that they too gain a lot from the experience.

Check Your Understanding

Answer the following questions about the Reading Passage.

1. Why are children in poorer families often unable to attend school?

2. Why might immigrant children struggle when attending schools in Japan?

3. According to the passage, which of the following is **NOT** considered "child labor"?
   a. Making clothing in a small room with no air conditioning or ventilation
   b. Working on their family's farm all day every day
   c. Being forced to beg for money in areas with many foreign tourists
   d. Occasionally helping out in their family's restaurant after school and on weekends

4. According to the passage, which of the following groups supports children who, for one reason or another, are struggling in Japan? (*You can circle more than one correct answer.*)
   a. Student volunteer groups
   b. NPOs
   c. Immigration officers
   d. Local governments

Vocabulary Review

Fill in the blanks with the words from the box below. Change the form of the words if necessary.

survey	struggle	slavery	recruit	abuse
be engaged	literacy	primary	immigrant	beneficial

1. Even though Japan's ____________________ rate is nearly 100 percent, the children of immigrants often have difficultiy reading and writing in Japanese.
2. Many children cannot go to school because they ____________________ in child labor.
3. ____________________ often have difficulties fitting into their new communities because they may not know the local language or culture.
4. Many children who cannot get an education are not only forced to work but also suffer from physical or sexual ____________________.
5. Exercise is ____________________ to your health.
6. I was never good at sports when I was young, so I always ____________________ in my physical education class.
7. Sadly, some children without parents are ____________________ as child soldiers.

Listening Comprehension

Listen to two students having a conversation at school. Use the words in the box below to complete the summary of the conversation.

DL 15

Preeda moved to Japan when she was 1.________________________ years old. She had a 2.________________________ at first because she couldn't understand Japanese. She couldn't talk with others and was 3.________________________ because she didn't have a nice *bento* lunch like her classmates did. Luckily, a woman in the community 4.________________________ to help Preeda and her family. She tutored Preeda and helped 5.________________________ with things like reading school notices and learning "*bento* culture." Because of her experience, Preeda decided to become 6.________________________.

hard time	angry	embarrassed
volunteered	good time	a teacher
six	her parents	eight

SDG 4: Quality Education

The aim of SDG 4 is to provide a good education for everyone. All children have the right to an education. However, many children cannot go to school, and girls especially have fewer opportunities to go to school than boys. Let's think more about why this unfortunate situation occurs.

Looking to the Future

The pictures below show some of the daytime activities done by some children in different countries. Think about the futures of the children shown in each of the pictures. What do you think will happen to them? Write a few sentences to explain your thoughts and discuss them with a partner.

Manual Labor

Studying at School

Fighting as a Child Soldier

My reaction

Action Cause and Effect Chain

In this activity, you will consider possible reasons as to why children in poorer countries cannot get an education and think about how the reasons relate to each other. Go to page 110 for details.

SDGs Quick Quiz

Can you guess the answer to the following SDGs-related question? Test your knowledge.

There are about two billion children in the world under the age of fifteen. About how many of them are estimated to live on the street or not to have a proper home?

a. 10 million (0.5 percent)
b. 40 million (2 percent)
c. 100 million (5 percent)
d. 150 million (8 percent)

Check your answer on page 110.

PART THREE

Multicultural Society

*Learning to live together, by developing an understanding
of other people and an appreciation of interdependence
—carrying out joint projects and learning to manage conflicts—
in a spirit of respect for the values of pluralism, mutual understanding and peace.*

UNESCO (1996) Learning: The Treasure Within

Chapter 8 Gender
Chapter 9 Refugees
Chapter 10 Insects

It is not easy to achieve the goal of leaving no one behind. There are some issues relating to specific groups that, so far, the SDGs have failed to address in a clear and meaningful way. Nevertheless, we need to create a world in which we can live together with respect for our differences. In this section, we will consider how we can expand the current SDGs by examining three topics: gender, refugees, and insects.

Daffodils
Meanings: Respect, Forgiveness

Chapter 8

Gender

Introduction

1. Do you want to get married in the future? If so, at what age do you want to get married?

2. What do you think about wearing school uniforms?
   Share your opinion with a partner.

Vocabulary List

Match the words with the definitions below. Look up the definition and review the synonyms.

No.	Word	Definition	Definition in my language	Synonyms
1	**terrible (adj.)**	h	ひどく嫌な、とても不快な	awful, horrible
2	**victim (n.)**			suffering person
3	**rite of passage (n.)**			adulthood, initiation
4	**inequality (n.)**			bias, unfairness
5	**salary (n.)**			income, wages
6	**gender (n.)**			sex
7	**identity (n.)**			character, personality
8	**consequence (n.)**			effect, result
9	**regardless of (adv.)**			in spite of, notwithstanding
10	**orientation (n)**			preference, position

Key: n. = noun, v. = verb, adj. = adjective, adv. = adverb

Definitions

a. someone who has suffered from the effects of violence, illness, or bad luck
b. the things that make a person or group of people unique
c. the social situation in which some people have more opportunities, money, etc., than others
d. a person's stance, viewpoint, preference, or nature
e. a fixed amount of money paid to an employee
f. the negative result of an action or situation
g. despite something
h. very bad, of low quality, or unpleasant
i. the physical and/or social condition of being male or female
j. a ceremony or activity that marks an important stage in a person's life, especially toward becoming recognized as an adult

Keyword: LGBT Community

There are various terms used to describe sexual orientation and gender identity, including "LGBT," "LGBTQ+," and "LGBTQIA," among others. This text uses "LGBT+" and "LGBT Community" as terms to respectfully encompass this diversity.

Reading Preview

Scan the Reading Passage and choose the paragraph number (1–5) that matches the pictures below.

(A) Paragraph No. ________

121st

(B) Paragraph No. ________

(C) Paragraph No. ________

(D) Paragraph No. ________

(E) Paragraph No. ________

Reading Passage

Being Respected Equally

DL 16

[1] Think back to when you were about ten years old. What did you enjoy doing? In many parts of the world, teenage girls and even girls as young as eight cannot enjoy a “normal” childhood because they are forced to marry and have children. According to UNICEF, there are currently about 650 million girls under the age of eighteen who are already married. Furthermore, the number of child marriages is increasing, especially in Africa. Because of poverty, some families force their daughters to marry to receive money in return. Can you imagine the **terrible** shock of finding out that you have been sold by your family?

[2] Women and girls are also more likely to face violence on a daily basis, or to become **victims** of trafficking. In some countries, young girls’ genitals are cut as a **rite of passage**. Women around the world face other **inequalities** in the form of gender discrimination. Even in the world’s most developed nations, women tend to have lower **salaries**, fewer employment opportunities, and less participation in public decision-making. For example, globally, women earn only about 80 percent of what men earn and make up only about one-quarter of national parliamentary members.

[3] Women are not the only ones who face discrimination because of their **gender**. LGBT+ is a collective term for lesbian, gay, bisexual, transgender, and other gender **identities**. Homosexuality is strictly prohibited in more than seventy countries. Some countries even apply

the death penalty for homosexuality. Furthermore, members of the LGBT community often face harsh discrimination and even violence around the world. Despite their vision of "leaving no one behind," the SDGs do not address LGBT+ discrimination as a gender issue because the countries that created them could not agree on it.

[4] What about gender issues in Japan? According to the World Gender Gap Report 2020, Japan ranks 121st out of 153 countries in gender equality. Japan received particularly bad marks for the lack of female participation in leadership roles. Moreover, Japan is the only country among the Group of Seven that does not give same-sex couples the same legal rights it gives to heterosexual couples. Even though it is estimated that about 10 percent of Japan's population are members of the LGBT community, very few people publicly "come out" because they are afraid of the potential **consequences** at home, work, or school.

[5] The first step we can take toward achieving gender equality is to reflect on what we already take for granted in our daily lives. We can do this by asking ourselves questions such as: Why are women usually expected to do the laundry? Why are women usually expected to wear skirts at work or at school? Why does the gender question in documents requiring ID often only have two options: male or female? By first recognizing such inequalities in our everyday lives, we can develop a new perspective and work to change them. **Regardless of** our gender or sexual **orientation**, we all deserve to be respected equally as individuals.

Check Your Understanding

Answer the following questions about the Reading Passage.

1. How is poverty related to child marriage?

2. How can asking questions about everyday situations help to achieve gender equality?

3. According to the passage, which of the following statements is **NOT** true of Japan?
   a. One hundred and twenty countries are considered to be more gender-equal than Japan.
   b. Japan is the only G7 member that discriminates against same-sex marriage.
   c. It is estimated that about 10 percent of the population is LGBT+.
   d. Women have equality in terms of leading the government.

4. According to the passage, what are women and girls more likely to suffer from? (*You can circle more than one correct answer.*)
   a. Trafficking
   b. Physical and sexual abuse
   c. Forced marriage
   d. Fewer employment opportunities

Vocabulary Review

Fill in the blanks with the words from the box below. Change the form of the words if necessary.

terrible	**victim**	**rite of passage**	**inequality**	**salary**
gender	**identity**	**consequence**	**regardless of**	**orientation**

1. People sometimes feel like they have lost their ______________________ after they retire.
2. The weather today is just ______________________. It has been pouring since this morning.
3. For many young people, getting a driver's license is a ______________________. It's an important step toward becoming an independent adult.
4. Takeshi didn't make as much money at his new job. However, despite the lower ______________________, he was much happier at work.
5. Sadly, women are often ______________________ of violence in their own homes.
6. One ______________________ of the recent hot weather is that there hasn't been enough rain for local crops.
7. Women occupying fewer positions of power than men is just one sign of gender ______________________.

Listening Comprehension

Listen to two students having a conversation at school. Use the words in the box below to complete the summary of the conversation.

DL 17

International Day of the Girl Child is 1.______________________ on October 11. On this day, people usually do things to 2.______________________ awareness of gender inequality. One example of this is the 3."______________________" movement, which aims to raise money for underprivileged girls. To 4.______________________ the movement on social media, people often take pictures of themselves holding 5.______________________ with a message that positively promotes women. Sally and James decide to make one and 6.______________________ together for a picture.

spread	**finish**	**raise**
celebrated	**Because I'm a Girl**	**a sign**
a flag	**pose**	**Think of the Girls**

SDG 5: Gender Equality

The aim of SDG 5 is to achieve gender equality and empower women and girls. This goal doesn't specifically refer to homosexual people and other members of the LGBT community. However, under the SDG's vision of "leaving no one behind," we need to aim for gender equality for *all* members of our society.

Recognizing Differences

The pictures below show the extent to which same-sex marriage is accepted in three different countries. Think about the differences between them. Write a few sentences to explain your thoughts and discuss them with a partner.

The Netherlands

Japan

Sudan

My reaction

Action Beyond Gender Stereotypes

In this activity, you will reflect on traditional gender stereotypes in your culture and how they make you feel. Go to page 111 for details.

SDGs Quick Quiz

Can you guess the answer to the following SDGs-related question? Test your knowledge.

In a survey of Japanese girls, what percentage responded that they "think women are better at cooking than men"?

a. 45 percent b. 55 percent c. 85 percent d. 95 percent

Check your answer on page 111.

Chapter 9
Refugees

Introduction

1. What words and images come to mind when you hear about refugees?

2. When one of your friends or family members is feeling down, what do you do to cheer them up?

Vocabulary List

Match the words with the definitions below. Look up the definition and review the synonyms.

No.	Word	Definition	Definition in my language	Synonyms
1	**refugee (n.)**	a	難民、避難者	displaced person
2	**persecute (v.)**			victimize, oppress
3	**flee (v.)**			run away, escape
4	**ongoing (adj.)**			continuing, current
5	**traumatic (adj.)**			painful, upsetting
6	**instantly (adv.)**			right away, without delay
7	**residency (n.)**			home
8	**grant (v.)**			bestow, give
9	**internal (adj.)**			inside, within
10	**compassionately (adv.)**			kindly, thoughtfully

Key: n. = noun, v. = verb, adj. = adjective, adv. = adverb

Definitions

a. someone who has been forced to leave their homeland, especially because of war or disasters
b. to give or allow someone something, usually in an official way
c. in a way that shows sympathy for others and a wish to help them
d. to treat people unfairly or cruelly because of their race, religion, or beliefs
e. the fact of living in a place
f. to leave a place quickly because you are in danger or are afraid
g. still happening
h. immediately, suddenly
i. existing or happening inside a person, organization, place, or country
j. making you feel shocked and upset

Reading Preview

Scan the Reading Passage and choose the paragraph number (1–5) that matches the pictures below.

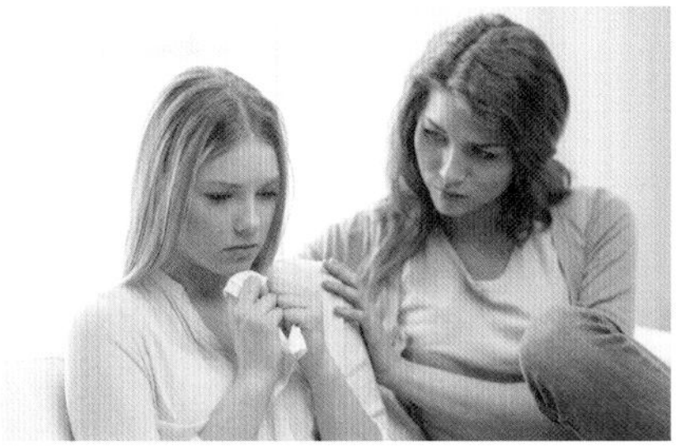

Fewer than 50 refugees a year

(A) Paragraph No. _______ (B) Paragraph No. _______ (C) Paragraph No. _______

(D) Paragraph No. _______ (E) Paragraph No. _______

Reading Passage

Forgotten by Society

DL 18

[1] If you've watched the news recently, you've probably seen stories about **refugees**. According to the United Nations, more than seventy million people worldwide are now refugees because of persecution and conflict. Very few of these refugees come to Japan because Japan usually only accepts fewer than fifty refugees a year. However, if we take time to look at the circumstances of refugees, we can appreciate not only how difficult their lives are but also how much we have in common with them.

[2] Refugees are often members of racial or religious minority groups. In Myanmar, for example, the Rohingya people were **persecuted** by the government. In 2017, the army burned down Rohingya villages, raped women, and killed thousands. As a result, about 850,000 people **fled** from their homes and into neighboring Bangladesh. Even today, these refugees cannot return to their home country. Furthermore, in addition to the **ongoing** suffering caused by their **traumatic** experience, they continue to struggle to adapt to life in underfunded refugee camps.

[3] Many people become refugees due to war and other conflicts. In 2011, a civil war began in Syria, killing nearly four hundred thousand people and injuring more than one million. About eleven million people—more than half of Syria's total population—became refugees as a result. Try to imagine what they experienced. Can you imagine **instantly** losing your home or even your family in an airstrike? How about living in a refugee camp where hunger or disease is

widespread? Even if we try, it can be hard to imagine how tough life is for displaced persons.

[4] Japan is generally closed to refugees, but there are still some living among us. For example, there are now more than two thousand Kurdish refugees living in Japan. However, because the Japanese government has never given them permission for permanent **residency**, some are forced to live in prison-like immigration facilities. Others are **granted** temporary permission to live outside of these facilities but are unable to legally work. Furthermore, there is another type of refugee in Japan you might not have considered: people who fled from their hometowns because of the nuclear accident or natural disasters. These "**internal** refugees" are also affected by fear, sadness, and uncertainty about their futures.

[5] Hannah Arendt, a German-Jewish philosopher, described refugees as people who have fallen into "holes of oblivion" and been forgotten by society. She argued that, in order to bring them out of these holes, we need to treat refugees as individuals and not just objects of pity. We probably all know people who have fallen into "holes of oblivion" through feelings of fear, loneliness, and loss, even if they are not refugees. By sitting down with and **compassionately** listening to people near us—friends, family, and neighbors—we can take the first step to ensure that refugees and those suffering from similar feelings of isolation are not forgotten.

Check Your Understanding

Answer the following questions about the Reading Passage.

1. Why did almost a million people flee from Myanmar in 2017?

2. Is it possible for people who are not refugees to experience feelings similar to those commonly felt by refugees?

3. According to the passage, which of the following statements is true of Kurdish refugees living in Japan?
   a. They are all forced to live in prison-like buildings.
   b. They are able to work freely.
   c. They are refugees who fled from natural disasters.
   d. They have not been given permission to live in Japan forever.

4. According to the passage, which of the following does **NOT** cause people to become refugees or internal refugees?
   a. Conflict and war
   b. Natural disasters
   c. Loss of income
   d. Religious persecution

Vocabulary Review

Fill in the blanks with the words from the box below. Change the form of the words if necessary.

refugee	**persecute**	**flee**	**ongoing**	**traumatic**
instantly	**residency**	**grant**	**internal**	**compassionately**

1. For refugees, it may be difficult to receive permission for permanent ____________________ from the Japanese government.
2. The Rohingya have been ____________________ because of their religious beliefs.
3. Ken ____________________ cried out in pain after he dropped the heavy book on his foot.
4. To be a good doctor, you need to be able to act ____________________ and professionally.
5. The death of a pet can be a ____________________ experience for a child.
6. To promote clean energy, the government will ____________________ a subsidy to all electric-car owners.
7. The large company created an ____________________ mailing system to make it easier for employees to send each other documents.

Listening Comprehension

Listen to two students having a conversation at school. Use the words in the box below to complete the summary of the conversation.

DL 19

Last weekend, Sally did some volunteer work in an area that was hit by a 1.____________________. She 2.____________________ with children whose parents were busy cleaning up their 3.____________________ homes. Sally said that the children were mostly just like 4.____________________ kids. However, Sally was worried about one little girl because she hardly 5.____________________. But at the end of the day, the little girl finally spoke up to say "6.____________________," which almost moved Sally to tears.

spoke	**typhoon**	**earthquake**
moved	**thank you**	**damaged**
normal	**spent time**	**new**

SDG 10: Reduced Inequalities

The aim of SDG 10 is to reduce inequality within and among countries. Due to differences in gender, ethnicity, and religion, many people suffer from discrimination and violence. People who move across borders, such as refugees and immigrants, are especially vulnerable and disadvantaged.

Making Connections

The pictures below show people in difficult situations. How do they connect with each other? Write a few sentences to explain your thoughts and discuss them with a partner.

Refugee Camp

Bullying

People Evacuating

My reaction

Action Where Do You Belong?

In this activity, you will be encouraged to think about people such as refugees who are often excluded from various groups. Go to page 112 for details.

SDGs Quick Quiz

Can you guess the answer to the following SDGs-related question? Test your knowledge.

In Japan, foreigners without legal residency status must leave Japan or be placed in immigrant facilities until they are granted permission to stay. What percentage of those living in such immigrant facilities live there for six months or longer?

a. 5 percent b. 14 percent c. 35 percent d. 54 percent

Check your answer on page 112.

Chapter 10

Insects

Introduction

1. Do you like insects and bugs? Which do you like? Which do you dislike?

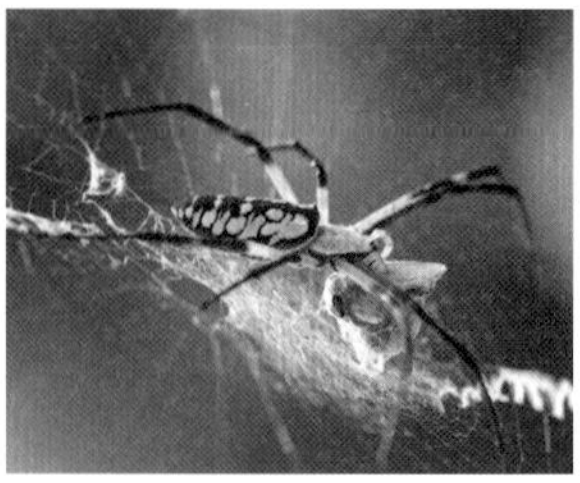

2. Did you know that insects are eaten in many countries? In which of the following countries is there a custom of eating insects?

   a. Mexico
   b. China
   c. Vietnam
   d. Japan
   e. South Africa

Vocabulary List

Match the words with the definitions below. Look up the definition and review the synonyms.

No.	Word	Definition	Definition in my language	Synonyms
1	**nuisance (n.)**	e	不愉快なもの、迷惑	bother, trouble
2	**reputation (n.)**			position, image
3	**vital (adj.)**			important, necessary
4	**hormone (n.)**			chemical
5	**organic (adj.)**			biological, natural
6	**essential (adj.)**			main, required
7	**pollinate (v.)**			fertilize
8	**pastime (n.)**			entertainment, hobby
9	**stinging (adj.)**			harsh, sharp
10	**pesticide (n.)**			chemical, poison

Key: n. = noun, v. = verb, adj. = adjective, adv. = adverb

Definitions

a. to take pollen from one plant to another so that new seeds can be produced
b. the general opinion, good or bad, that people have about someone or something
c. coming from a living organism
d. making you feel a short, sharp, unpleasant sensation
e. someone or something that annoys you or causes trouble for you
f. necessary or needed
g. an activity that is done for enjoyment
h. a chemical substance used to kill harmful insects and plants
i. necessary or very important in terms of something's existence
j. any of the various chemicals in the body that influence its growth and how it works

Reading Preview

Scan the Reading Passage and choose the paragraph number (1–5) that matches the pictures below.

(A) Paragraph No. _______

Nutrition ⇧
Cost ⇩

(B) Paragraph No. _______

(C) Paragraph No. _______

(D) Paragraph No. _______

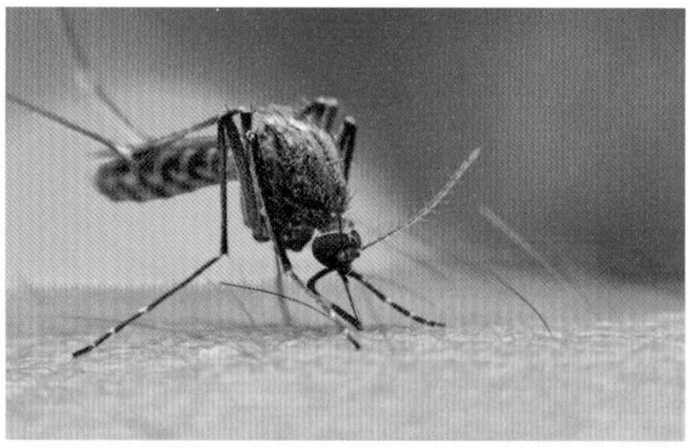

(E) Paragraph No. _______

Reading Passage

Insects: Earth's Smallest Heroes

DL 20

[1] When you close your eyes and imagine an insect, what comes to mind? Most people will immediately think of **nuisances** such as cockroaches and mosquitos, or of other "creepy" bugs like spiders. However, despite their negative **reputation**, the planet's one million species of insects and bugs are all important to our lives. Not only do they play a **vital** role in sustaining the environment and global economy, but they also offer a possible solution to the world's hunger problem.

[2] Insects are edible and are a much more efficient source of nutrition than animal-based products. Animals need a lot of grain and other resources (such as land) for feeding. In addition, meat products can harbor disease or be filled with **hormones** and chemicals. Insects, on the other hand, consume very little and can eat a variety of **organic** materials. They don't need much space, are inexpensive to keep, and reproduce quickly. They are also nutritious, containing high quantities of protein, fat, and other nutrients. In fact, the WHO has declared that insects have the potential to help solve the world's hunger crisis.

[3] Insects contribute to our lives and to the environment in other ways, too. Silkworms, for example, can not only be eaten but also produce silk. The production and sale of silk products is a major part of the economy in many countries. Bees are **essential** to maintaining the environment, as they **pollinate** flowers and plants, including fruits and vegetables eaten

by people all over the world. Insects are vital to our lives, but recently, they have started to disappear. Studies have found that 40 percent of insect species are now declining, and the rate at which bees are dying has drastically increased. Scientists still do not know precisely why this is happening.

[4] Insects also play a crucial role in our everyday lives in Japan. Fruits pollinated by insects are consumed by people all over the country every day and make up a major part of many local economies. Insects are also important to Japanese culture. Traditional dishes such as *hachinoko* (bee larvae) are still prized for their unique flavors and nutritional benefits, and hunting for beetles and dragonflies is a favorite childhood **pastime**. Summer in Japan just wouldn't be the same without the **stinging** cry of the cicada. Can you imagine life in Japan without insects?

[5] You may be surprised to know there are many ways in which you can help to protect this important part of our ecosystem and culture. One thing you can do is to start a "bee-friendly" garden by planting a wide variety of pollen-producing flowers. You could also try to buy food that was grown without the use of **pesticides**. Other options include supporting local beekeepers by purchasing their honey, or donating to organizations that work for bee conservation. It's still not too late for us to create an insect-friendly world and a society committed to biodiversity and the enjoyment of its fruits!

Check Your Understanding

Answer the following questions about the Reading Passage.

1. Why are insects seen as a possible solution to the world's hunger crisis?

2. In addition to being a possible food source, what are some of the other ways in which insects contribute to our lives?

3. According to the passage, which of the following is **NOT** an effective way to protect insects?
   a. Using pesticides to kill unwanted insects like mosquitos and cockroaches
   b. Buying honey from local beekeepers
   c. Making a "bee-friendly" garden
   d. Buying fresh produce that was grown without the use of chemicals

4. According to the passage, why are so many insects around the world starting to disappear?
   a. Too many people are eating them.
   b. They are being killed off by bugs like spiders and centipedes.
   c. Science has not yet identified the reason.
   d. They are being eaten by animals that are later killed for their meat.

Vocabulary Review

Fill in the blanks with the words from the box below. Change the form of the words if necessary.

nuisance	**reputation**	**vital**	**hormone**	**organic**
essential	**pollinate**	**pastime**	**stinging**	**pesticide**

1. Bees are a ____________________ part of the process of producing many fruits and vegetables.
2. My neighbor is such a ____________________! He always plays loud music late at night.
3. ____________________ are given to animals intended for human consumption, such as cows and chickens, to make them grow quickly.
4. Playing baseball is a popular ____________________, especially in the United States and Japan.
5. That hotel has a bad ____________________. You shouldn't stay there.
6. Scientists think that many bees are dying because they are being poisoned by ____________________.
7. Water is ____________________ to life. Humans, for example, can only survive a few days without water.

Listening Comprehension

Listen to two students having a conversation at school. Use the words in the box below to complete the summary of the conversation.

DL 21

During her summer vacation, Mako visited 1.____________________ in Nagano. While she was there, she ate bee larvae, a 2.____________________ delicacy. Mako tells James that insects can be used 3.____________________ world hunger. However, one big 4.____________________ is making insects attractive to customers, because many people can't 5.____________________ the disturbing mental image of eating insects. James says that he is open 6.____________________ it.

issue	**to solve**	**her relatives**
her friends	**solution**	**modern**
get past	**traditional**	**to trying**

SDG15: Life on Land

The aim of SDG 15 is to protect life on land. Human life is supported by Mother Nature. Therefore, we should preserve forests, prevent desertification, and stop biodiversity loss. Insects are an important part of our biodiversity, and our lives would not be the same without them.

Looking to the Future

The pictures below show some of the possible consequences if bees disappear from the Earth. How should we face these problems? Write a few sentences to explain your thoughts and discuss them with a partner.

No Honey

Expensive Fruits and Vegetables

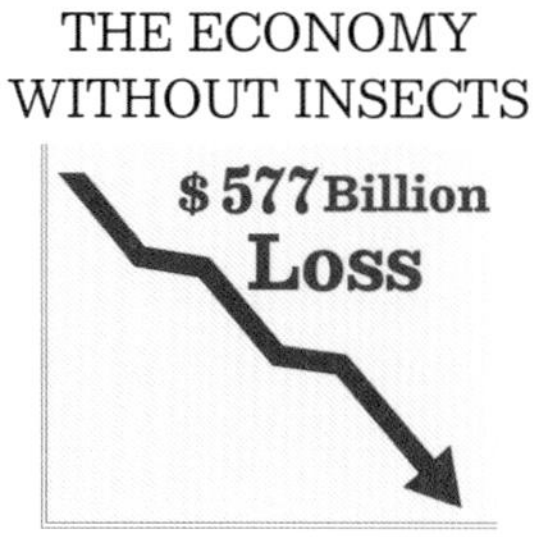

Downturn in the Global Economy

My reaction

Action Insects and Memories from Childhood

In this activity, you will think about some of your childhood memories relating to insects and use those memories as a basis for interaction. Go to page 113 for details.

SDGs Quick Quiz

Can you guess the answer to the following SDGs-related question? Test your knowledge.

What percentage of the one hundred most common food crops are pollinated by bees?

a. 40 percent b. 50 percent c. 60 percent d. 70 percent

Check your answer on page 113.

PART FOUR

Action for Change

The changes can be a process of re-orientation of habitual action at the individual level, and/or a process of change at the level of the community as the system.

UNESCO (2014) Global Citizenship Education:
Preparing Learners for the Challenges of the 21st Century

Chapter 11 Vegetarianism
Chapter 12 Plastic Waste
Chapter 13 Shopping

The preceding chapters have taught us that we can tackle any global issues through our day-to-day actions. This section will similarly emphasize the point that we can all make a significant difference by making small adjustments in our daily lives. In order to explore this great potential, we will consider the following three topics: vegetarianism, plastic waste, and shopping.

Chrysanthemums
Meaning: Hope for the future

Chapter 11

Vegetarianism

Introduction

1. What are some of the reasons why people become vegetarians? Think about possible reasons and share them with a partner.

2. If you were to stop eating all animal products (including meat, eggs, milk, and cheese), which foods would you miss the most?

Vocabulary List

Match the words with the definitions below. Look up the definition and review the synonyms.

No.	Word	Definition	Definition in my language	Synonyms
1	**vegetarian (n.)**	b	菜食主義者、ベジタリアン	plant-eater
2	**dairy (adj.)**			milk-based
3	**citizen (n.)**			national, resident
4	**suitable (adj.)**			acceptable, fitting
5	**graze (v.)**			eat, feed
6	**well-being (n.)**			health, happiness
7	**mass-produced (adj.)**			factory-assembled, manufactured
8	**additive (n.)**			addition, supplement
9	**moderation (n.)**			patience, restraint
10	**waistline (n.)**			gut, midsection

Key: n. = noun, v. = verb, adj. = adjective, adv. = adverb

Definitions

a. refers to foods that are made from milk, such as butter, cream, and cheese
b. someone who does not eat meat or fish
c. acceptable or a good match for someone or something
d. created cheaply and in large numbers using machines in a factory
e. a person who lives as an accepted member of society in a particular place
f. the quality of doing something within reasonable limits
g. something added to food to improve it or to preserve it
h. the measured size of the middle area of your body
i. to eat grass
j. the state of feeling healthy and happy

Reading Preview

Scan the Reading Passage and choose the paragraph number (1–5) that matches the pictures below.

(A) Paragraph No. _______

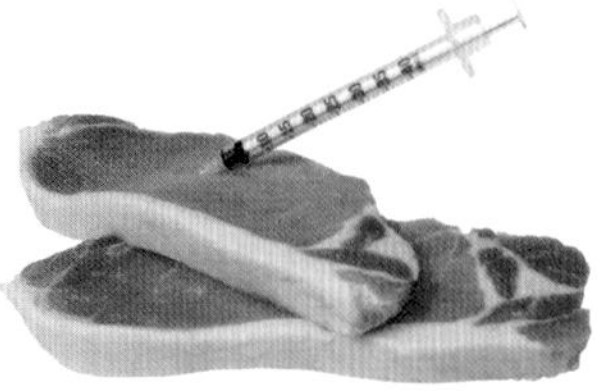

(B) Paragraph No. _______

(C) Paragraph No. _______

(D) Paragraph No. _______

(E) Paragraph No. _______

Reading Passage

Our Food Choices and the World Around Us

DL 22

[1] Recently, vegetarianism has become more common as a lifestyle choice. Vegans are **vegetarians** who choose not to eat *any* products that come from animals, not just meat but also eggs and **dairy** products. Can you imagine having such a diet? Chances are that many of your favorite foods contain animal products. Although becoming a vegan or vegetarian can be difficult, recently more people are doing it because they feel it's their responsibility as "global **citizens**." Let's explore some of the reasons why.

[2] One reason relates to animal welfare. Many people feel that animals have similar rights to humans, so they do not want to support industries that cause animals to suffer. Egg-laying hens, for example, often spend their lives in small cages no wider than an A4-sized sheet of paper. Their cages are so small that the hens often injure themselves, suffering from broken bones and cuts. Males cannot lay eggs and are not **suitable** for meat, so they are generally killed soon after hatching. Furthermore, dairy cows are kept in a state of pregnancy so that they can always produce milk. Once they can no longer produce enough milk, they are usually killed.

[3] Another reason why people choose to become vegetarians is because of the negative impact animal farming has upon the environment. A major reason for deforestation is the desire to make room for animals to **graze**, and to create crops for animal feed. In fact, about 70 percent of the land lost from the Amazon rainforest is now being used for these purposes. Surprisingly, animals also contribute to climate change. It is estimated that about 15 percent

of all greenhouse gases are produced by livestock. In addition, raising animals can require up to ten times the amount of water needed to grow wheat. These water resources could be used much more efficiently, especially in areas where fresh water is limited.

[4] Finally, many people choose to avoid eating meat because of how it affects human health and **well-being**. Raising livestock makes grain unaffordable to many people in poorer parts of the world, greatly contributing to the global hunger problem. Furthermore, **mass-produced** animal products often contain hormones and other chemical **additives** that may negatively affect our health. Such additives have been linked to higher rates of disease and to hormone imbalances, among other health problems.

[5] It is clear that our eating habits are negatively affecting the world around us. However, it is unrealistic to expect people to suddenly change. Even if we don't all become vegetarians, we can still take small steps to make our diets more socially responsible. We can, for example, try to eat more traditional Japanese meals that are mainly made up of vegetables and other non-meat products. Or we can change our diets to be more "flexitarian," which means eating mostly plant-based foods with animal products only being eaten in **moderation**. At the very least, next time we go food shopping, we should think about more than our **waistlines** when considering what to buy.

Check Your Understanding

Answer the following questions about the Reading Passage.

1. What are three reasons why a person might become a vegetarian?

2. What is the difference between a vegan diet and a flexitarian diet?

3. According to the passage, which of the following statements does **NOT** refer to a way in which the production of animal products negatively affects the environment?
   a. Animals produce greenhouse gases, contributing to climate change.
   b. Fresh water resources are used inefficiently to feed animals.
   c. Grazing animals eat tree roots, causing damage to the rainforest.
   d. Natural landscapes, such as forests, are destroyed to make room for animal production.

4. According to the passage, on large farms, what happens to animals that cannot produce milk or eggs?
   a. They are sold to local farmers.
   b. They are frequently killed.
   c. They are given hormones to help them produce again.
   d. They are left to live until they die of natural causes.

Vocabulary Review

Fill in the blanks with the words from the box below. Change the form of the words if necessary.

vegetarian	**dairy**	**citizen**	**suitable**	**graze**
well-being	**mass-produced**	**additive**	**moderation**	**waistline**

1. ____________________ keep certain foods fresh, so they are often used in convenience store meals.
2. Plastic bags are ____________________ because they are cheap to make and extremely useful.
3. It's okay to eat junk food in ____________________.
4. I noticed that you haven't been eating much recently. Are you worried about your ____________________?
5. I absolutely love ____________________ products. Ice cream is my favorite!
6. Much of the Amazon rainforest has been cut down to create land for animals to ____________________.
7. If you're worried about your friend's ____________________, you should give him a call.

Listening Comprehension

Listen to two students having a conversation at school. Use the words in the box below to complete the summary of the conversation.

DL 23

James has noticed that Sally never eats meat for 1.____________________. She explains that it's because farms inject hormones and 2.____________________ into animals. She tells James that she's a 3.____________________, which is someone who has a mostly vegetarian diet but who still eats meat in moderation. Sally limits her meat consumption by only eating it 4.____________________. She also only buys "organic" meat that comes from livestock that has been 5.____________________ without added chemicals or hormones. Finally, she tells James about 6.____________________, a campaign that encourages people to choose one day a week and not to eat meat on that day.

Meatless Mondays	**raised**	**once a month**
lunch	**chemicals**	**flexitarian**
once a day	**Meatless Sundays**	**dinner**

SDG 3: Good Health and Well-being

The aim of SDG 3 is to promote the good health and well-being of people of all ages. There are various reasons why vegetarians choose not to eat meat. Let's try to understand how vegetarians think and how their eating habits can benefit the future health of all living things.

Recognizing Differences

The pictures below show some of the reasons why vegetarians don't eat meat. Which reasons, if any, do you agree with? Choose one or more, then write a few sentences to explain your thoughts and discuss them with a partner.

Animal Welfare

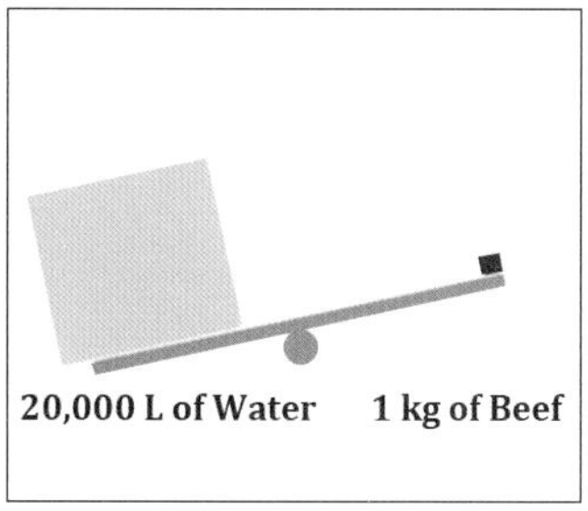

Water Waste

Hunger

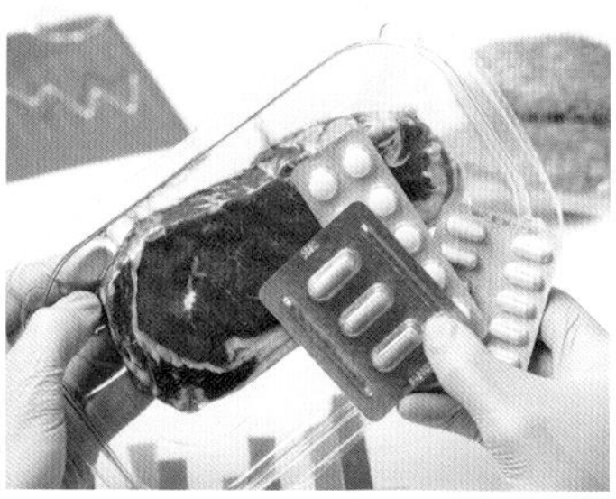

Health Concerns

My reaction

Action Making Advertisements

In this activity, you will be encouraged to consider conflicting viewpoints on animal welfare. You will learn the importance of forming your own opinions in our complicated world. Go to page 114 for details.

SDGs Quick Quiz

Can you guess the answers to the following SDGs-related questions? Test your knowledge.

What percentage of people in Japan are vegetarian? What percentage of people have a flexitarian diet and, therefore, consciously reduce their consumption of animal products on one or more days of the week? Circle two answers below (one for each question).

a. Less than 1 percent b. 3.8 percent c. 5.7 percent d. 19.8 percent

Check your answers on page 114.

Chapter 12

Plastic Waste

Introduction

1. Look around you for things that do not contain any plastic. What can you find?

2. How many plastic bottles do you use in a year? (Think about how many bottles you use in an average week and multiply it by fifty-two.) Share your answer with your classmates. Who had the highest number? Who had the lowest?

Vocabulary List

Match the words with the definitions below. Look up the definition and review the synonyms.

No.	Word	Definition	Definition in my language	Synonyms
1	**durable (adj.)**	c	長持ちする、丈夫な	lasting, strong
2	**dispose (v.)**			throw away, discard
3	**decompose (v.)**			break down, fall apart
4	**tangled (adj.)**			knotted, trapped
5	**originate (v.)**			come from, result
6	**urgent (adj.)**			demanding, immediate
7	**ban (v.)**			stop, prevent
8	**restrict (v.)**			limit, regulate
9	**per capita (adj., adv.)**			per head, per person
10	**threaten (v.)**			endanger

Key: n. = noun, v. = verb, adj. = adjective, adv. = adverb

Definitions

a. to refuse to allow something, especially in an official way
b. very important and in need of immediate attention
c. able to be used or to continue to exist for a long time
d. to be likely to cause harm or damage to something or someone
e. to separate or break into smaller and smaller parts over time
f. twisted together in a disordered way
g. to limit one's actions or movements, or the size or amount of something
h. to come from a particular place, time, or situation
i. to get rid of something, especially by throwing it away
j. for or by each person

Reading Preview

Scan the Reading Passage and choose the paragraph number (1–5) that matches the pictures below.

(A) Paragraph No. ______

(B) Paragraph No. ______

(C) Paragraph No. ______

(D) Paragraph No. ______

(E) Paragraph No. ______

Reading Passage

Killing Our Oceans

DL 24

[1] Look around you and count how many things you can see that contain plastic. There are probably a lot. Plastic has become such an important part of daily life that it's hard to imagine life without it. Plastic is light, **durable**, and water-resistant. Moreover, it's cheap and easy to produce. Even though it seems like plastic is a "miracle material," it cannot be easily **disposed** of. It can take a thousand years for a piece of plastic to **decompose**, and burning plastic produces harmful gases, contributing to climate change.

[2] Plastic waste has had a major impact on ecosystems, especially the ocean. It is estimated that at least eight million tons of plastic trash is dumped into the ocean every year. Shockingly, it is predicted that by 2050, there will be as much plastic as there are fish in the ocean. Some of this plastic ends up being eaten by marine life. In recent years, many dead whales, turtles, and other animals have been found with their stomachs full of plastic. Plastic may also harm animals by getting **tangled** around them or blocking their breathing.

[3] The dangers caused by plastic waste go beyond what we can easily see. Microplastics are pieces of plastic that are smaller than five millimeters. They **originate** from larger pieces of plastic that have broken down over time. These tiny pieces of plastic are not only consumed by sea animals and other animals such as birds, but also by humans. According to the WWF, the average person eats five grams of microplastics—or the equivalent of one credit card—*every*

week. It is still not clear what effect this has on our bodies, but it is thought to increase the risk of diseases such as cancer.

[4] Slowly, countries around the world are starting to realize how **urgent** this problem is. In the early 2000s, some developing countries such as Bangladesh and Rwanda were the first to create laws **banning** some single-use plastics. Many countries, including Japan, have since followed suit. Even so, Japan still produces about nine million tons (roughly the weight of sixty thousand jumbo jets) of plastic trash annually and burns about 70 percent of it. Much of the remaining trash is shipped to China and other countries. However, as these countries begin to **restrict** plastic imports, Japan is running out of options as to what to do with its plastic waste.

[5] Most plastic waste comes from single-use plastic, and Japan has the second-worst plastic packaging waste **per capita** in the world. Luckily, this is one problem where we, as individuals, can make a big difference. Just by using reusable bottles and bags, and by avoiding single-use plastics, we can help solve the problem. Perhaps more importantly, we should speak out against wasteful plastic use to encourage companies and local governments to lower their dependency on single-use plastic. Together we can create an environment in which animals and people can safely eat and drink without the risk of consuming life-**threatening** plastic.

Check Your Understanding

Answer the following questions about the Reading Passage.

1. Why is it so difficult to dispose of plastic waste?

2. What are microplastics, and where do they come from?

3. According to the passage, which of the following statements is true of plastic trash?
   a. There is less microplastic in the oceans around Japan than there is in the oceans around most other island countries.
   b. Japan can easily ship its plastic trash to other countries.
   c. There will be as much plastic trash as fish in the ocean by 2050.
   d. While many sea animals accidentally eat plastic, humans do not.

4. According to the passage, which of the following is **NOT** suggested as a way to solve the plastic problem?
   a. Using reusable bags
   b. Not using credit cards
   c. Encouraging companies to reduce their consumption of single-use plastic
   d. Avoiding buying single-use plastic

Vocabulary Review

Fill in the blanks with the words from the box below. Change the form of the words if necessary.

durable	dispose	decompose	tangled	originate
urgent	ban	restrict	per capita	threaten

1. Citrus fruits ____________________ in China and Southeast Asia.
2. Cars need to be made of ____________________ materials in order to prevent them from breaking or falling apart.
3. Kim's boss needed to talk with her right away. It was ____________________.
4. Plastic waste in the ocean ____________________ sea animals because it can make them sick or even cause them to die.
5. I try to ____________________ myself to one cup of coffee a day. If I drink any more than that, I have trouble sleeping at night.
6. It takes about a thousand years for plastic bags to ____________________.
7. Airlines have ____________________ smoking on airplanes to prevent the risk of fire.

Listening Comprehension

Listen to two students having a conversation at school. Use the words in the box below to complete the summary of the conversation.

DL 25

James was 1.____________________ the first time he went to a grocery store in Japan because of the way the fruits and vegetables were 2.____________________. He thinks the individual wrapping is 3.____________________ and that it doesn't match with his 4. ____________________ of *mottainai* culture in Japan. Mako suggests saying something to the store by using the 5.____________________ box. James says that he is getting 6.____________________ and suggests going to the store together.

excited	customer feedback	wasteful
surprised	understanding	hungry
efficient	complaint	packaged

14 LIFE BELOW WATER

SDG 14: Life below Water

The aim of SDG 14 is to protect life below water. In order to achieve this goal, we must reduce the amount of waste that goes into the oceans and reconsider how we use our marine resources. Reducing plastic waste is one change we can immediately make in our daily lives.

Making Connections

The pictures below show some of the problems created by plastic waste over time. Think about how they connect with each other. Write a few sentences to explain your thoughts and discuss them with a partner.

Harmful Gases / Global Warming

PLASTIC WASTE
TOP3
①U.S.A.
②Japan
③E.U.

Exporters of Plastic Waste

Animal Suffering

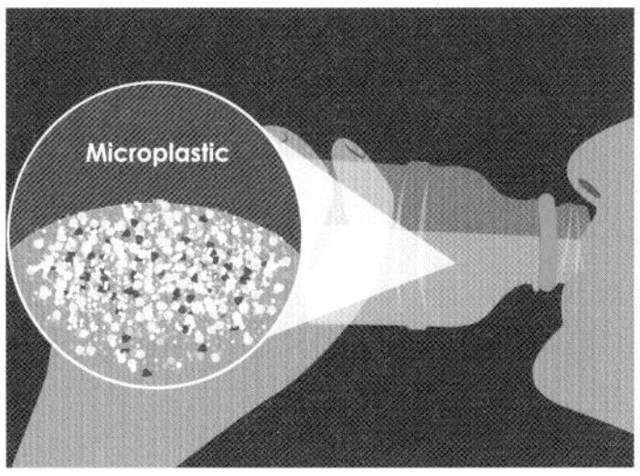

Microplastic

My reaction

Action Plastic Waste Campaign

In this activity, you will think about ways to reduce plastic waste and create a campaign with your classmates to share your ideas with others. Go to page 115 for details.

SDGs Quick Quiz

Can you guess the answer to the following SDGs-related question? Test your knowledge.

In accordance with the Basel Convention, the export of plastic waste will be banned from 2021. About how much plastic waste does Japan export every year?

a. Fifty thousand tons
b. Two hundred thousand tons
c. Five hundred thousand tons
d. One million tons

Check your answer on page 115.

Chapter 13

Shopping

Introduction

1. Do you like shopping? What kind of things do you like to buy?

2. Have you ever seen this logo before? What do you think it means?

FAIRTRADE

Vocabulary List

Match the words with the definitions below. Look up the definition and review the synonyms.

No.	Word	Definition	Definition in my language	Synonyms
1	**pillar (n.)**	b	柱、中心となるもの	support, foundation
2	**quantity (n.)**			amount
3	**survival (n.)**			continuation
4	**awareness (n.)**			attention, understanding
5	**sacrifice (v.)**			give up, let go
6	**emphasize (v.)**			highlight, stress
7	**prioritize (v.)**			arrange, prefer
8	**certify (v.)**			confirm, approve
9	**ethical (adj.)**			correct, moral
10	**essentially (adv.)**			basically, centrally

Key: n. = noun, v. = verb, adj. = adjective, adv. = adverb

Definitions

a. to give up something that is valuable to you in order to achieve something
b. someone or something very important to a place or organization
c. relating to what is right or wrong
d. to state in a formal or official way that something is true, has authority, or has been approved
e. to decide upon what is most important so that you can deal with it first
f. how much or how many there is of something
g. in a basic way
h. the mental state of knowing about something or understanding something
i. continuing to live or exist, especially after experiencing a difficult or dangerous situation
j. to show that something is especially important or needs special attention

Study Tip

The suffix **-ize** is often added to adjectives and nouns in order to turn them into verbs.

Noun	*Verb*	*Adjective*	*Verb*
Priority	*Priorit**ize***	*Actual*	*Actual**ize***
Emphasis	*Emphas**ize***	*Final*	*Final**ize***
Apology	*Apolog**ize***	*American*	*American**ize***

Reading Preview

Scan the Reading Passage and choose the paragraph number (1–5) that matches the pictures below.

(A) Paragraph No. _______

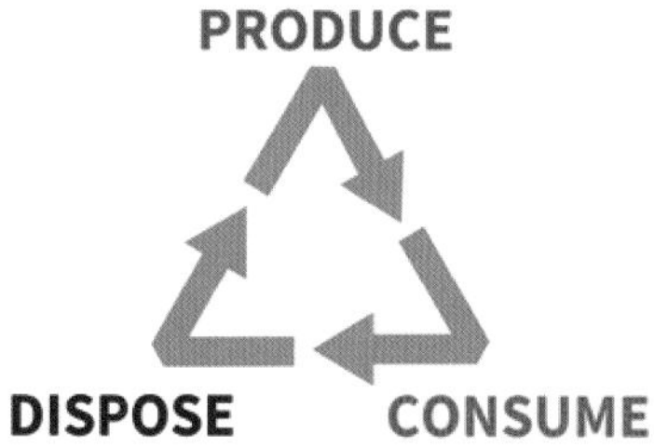

(B) Paragraph No. _______

(C) Paragraph No. _______

(D) Paragraph No. _______

Ethical Consumption

(E) Paragraph No. _______

Reading Passage

Can We Buy Happiness?

DL 26

[1] Shopping can make us feel happy. Whether we are buying clothes at the mall or getting the latest smartphone, shopping is something most people enjoy. It is a major part of our lives and a driving force that moves the global economy. But just how much do we shop? You may be surprised to learn that shopping for personal consumption makes up more than 50 percent of Japan's GDP. It is often thought that Japan's financial strength is based on exports. However, personal consumption—our daily shopping—is perhaps the single most important **pillar** supporting Japan's economy.

[2] Modern society produces, consumes, and disposes of a large **quantity** of materials. This cycle of mass-consumption provides us with convenient and comfortable lives. However, it also negatively affects the natural environment and threatens our **survival**. To raise **awareness** of this danger, the Ecological Footprint was created as a way of calculating each individual's impact upon the environment. For example, if everyone on Earth had the same consumption habits as the average American, the Ecological Footprint data tells us that we would need more than five Earths to sustain the human race.

[3] Beyond its effect on the environment, our mass-consumer society also affects what we buy and from whom we buy it. As consumers, we generally want to buy things as cheaply as possible but without **sacrificing** quality. However, we rarely think about the people who produce what we buy or their working conditions. Many of the everyday items we buy may be

produced by children or other vulnerable members of society. They may be laboring in terrible working environments for very low wages. For example, when you buy a cup of coffee for three hundred and thirty yen, only about two yen actually goes to the producer.

[4] The Fair Trade movement aims to correct this type of economic inequality. In ordinary trade, the sellers aim to make as much profit as possible by making their products as cheaply as possible and selling them at a high price. Fair Trade, on the other hand, **emphasizes** paying fair prices for raw materials and products from developing countries. It **prioritizes** helping the producers in developing countries become independent. Support organizations such as Fairtrade International have issued certification labels and made efforts to spread Fair Trade globally. In addition, there are now over two thousand **certified** "Fair Trade Towns" around the world, including six cities in Japan.

[5] "**Ethical** consumption" is a term for consumer behavior that focuses on people, communities, and the environment. It is a way to improve the world through our shopping and help us be mindful of what we buy. Examples of ethical consumption are Fair Trade, eco-friendly products, recycled products, and products that support people in disaster-hit areas. **Essentially**, ethical consumption means thinking about the environment and people other than yourself when you shop. It shows us that, by connecting our shopping habits and global issues, we can contribute to making the world a better place.

Check Your Understanding

Answer the following questions about the Reading Passage.

1. How does Fair Trade help overcome economic inequality?

2. What is "ethical consumption"?

3. According to the passage, which of the following statements is true about the "Ecological Footprint"?
   a. It tells us that Americans produce more than five times more waste than the rest of the world combined.
   b. It enables people to measure how they personally affect the environment.
   c. It is one of the most important pillars of Japan's economy.
   d. It damages our environment.

4. According to the passage, which of the following is **NOT** affected by our shopping habits?
   a. The environment
   b. The economic situations of people in developing countries
   c. Children working in poor conditions in Japan
   d. Japan's economy

Vocabulary Review

Fill in the blanks with the words from the box below. Change the form of the words if necessary.

pillar	quantity	survival	awareness	sacrifice
emphasize	prioritize	certify	ethical	essentially

1. Global warming threatens the ____________________ of millions of species of animals all over the planet.
2. It's important for students to learn how to ____________________. In other words, they must decide which tasks are more deserving of their time and energy.
3. Scientists ____________________ the importance of wearing masks to prevent the spread of COVID-19.
4. Some people choose not to eat meat for ____________________ reasons. In other words, they think that it's wrong to kill animals for food.
5. Watching the news regularly is one way to increase your ____________________ of global events.
6. The mayor was a ____________________ of her local community. She helped people in need and was loved by everyone.
7. One reason why plastic is so cheap is that it can be produced quickly and in large ____________________.

Listening Comprehension

Listen to two students having a conversation at school. Use the words in the box below to complete the summary of the conversation.

DL 27

James has been thinking about his 1.__________________________ recently. He tells Sally about 2.__________________________. It takes place on Black Friday and encourages people not to buy unnecessary things or 3.__________________________ resources. James and Sally decide to create a similar day that is dedicated to buying things for 4.__________________________. Instead of buying something that one of them wants, they will buy something that someone else actually 5.__________________________. They decide to call this new day "Buying It 6.__________________________ Day."

needs	others	myself
shopping habits	save	waste
Buy Nothing Day	wants	Forward

12 RESPONSIBLE CONSUMPTION AND PRODUCTION

SDG 12: Responsible Consumption and Production

The aim of SDG 12 is to ensure sustainable consumption and production. Mass production and consumption have caused various global problems, such as a lack of resources, climate change, and excessive waste. Through ethical consumption, we can help solve these problems.

Looking to the Future

Imagine that you are shopping. Which of the following ethical consumption products would you choose to make our world a better place? Write a few sentences to explain your choice and discuss it with a partner.

Organic Cotton T-shirt

Recycled Products

Local Specialties

My reaction

Action Buying It Forward

In this activity, you will think about your shopping habits and about creative ways you could use your purchasing power to help people in need. Go to page 116 for details.

SDGs Quick Quiz

Can you guess the answer to the following SDGs-related question? Test your knowledge.

Six cities in Japan are certified as Fair Trade Towns. Which city became the first Fair Trade Town both in Japan and in all of Asia in 2011?

a. Sapporo b. Kyoto c. Nagoya d. Kumamoto

Check your answer on page 116.

EPILOGUE

Continuing the Journey

While the journey outwards leads students to discover the world in which they live, the journey inwards heightens their understanding of themselves and of their potential.

G. Pike & D. Selby (1999) In the Global Classroom

Chapter 14 Partnerships

Learning is often compared to an endless journey.
Similarly, the journey toward becoming a global citizen has no final destination.
Even the SDGs will continue to evolve as they adapt to new challenges and new demands.
In this final section, we, the authors, will leave you with a question:
As a global citizen, with whom would you like to travel along the road
toward a fairer, more peaceful world?

White Roses
Meaning: New beginnings

Chapter 14

Partnerships

Introduction

1. What does the word "partnership" mean to you? Share your thoughts with a partner.

2. In this unit, we will be considering how the COVID-19 virus changed our world in 2020. How did the pandemic affect you personally? Share your experiences with a partner.

Vocabulary List

Match the words with the definitions below. Look up the definition and review the synonyms.

No.	Word	Definition	Definition in my language	Synonyms
1	**pandemic (n.)**	h	深刻な感染病の大流行	disease, outbreak
2	**sphere (n.)**			domain, field
3	**exception (n.)**			exclusion, omission
4	**partnership (n.)**			cooperation, sharing
5	**significance (n.)**			importance, merit
6	**anxiety (n.)**			concern, worry
7	**hoard (v.)**			keep, stock
8	**descent (n.)**			ancestry, origin
9	**desperate (adj.)**			critical, urgent
10	**determine (v.)**			control, decide

Key: n. = noun, v. = verb, adj. = adjective, adv. = adverb

Definitions

a. something that is not included or is different
b. to keep a large number of things for one's own benefit
c. a range or area of activity
d. relating to one's lineage or family background
e. very serious or bad
f. to decide what will happen or to control the outcome
g. importance; special meaning
h. a dangerous disease that spreads quickly across a large region and infects many people
i. an uncomfortable feeling of nervousness or about something that might happen
j. an agreement between two or more organizations, people, etc., to work together

Reading Preview

Scan the Reading Passage and choose the paragraph number (1–5) that matches the pictures below.

(A) Paragraph No. _______

(B) Paragraph No. _______

(C) Paragraph No. _______

(D) Paragraph No. _______

(E) Paragraph No. _______

Reading Passage

Together in the Face of Disaster

DL 28

[1] In 2020, the WHO declared that the spread of a new virus, known as COVID-19, had become a global **pandemic**. In just a few months, the deadly virus had spread around the world, causing hundreds of thousands of people to lose their lives. In a sense, we now live in a single "global **sphere**" in which everything, including people, things, and information, can quickly travel across national borders. Disease is no **exception**. In our globalized society, people now spread diseases more quickly and further afield than ever before.

[2] The seventeenth and final goal of the SDGs is to form and strengthen "global **partnerships**." This is seen as the key to achieving the 169 targets. People from around the globe will need to connect with each other, overcome their differences, and take action for the future. If we do nothing, the problems described by the SDGs will worsen, and it will be too late for the next generation to take effective action. Let's examine the world's response to the COVID-19 pandemic and think about what it can teach us about the meaning and **significance** of making global partnerships.

[3] The effects of the pandemic were psychological as well as physical. The fear and **anxiety** divided people and created barriers between them. Some people selfishly **hoarded** masks, toilet paper, and other necessities, thereby preventing vulnerable people from getting access to them. Meanwhile, in many countries, people of Asian **descent**, sick people, and even medical workers found themselves facing discrimination as some other people closed their hearts in

fear. In an already **desperate** situation, this type of behavior only made things worse.

[4] The COVID-19 pandemic has, however, served to emphasize the central message behind the SDGs: "no one will be left behind." In a pandemic, the only way to control the spread of a disease and ultimately overcome it is to create partnerships. After all, even if one country were to be successful in stopping the spread of the virus, that achievement would be meaningless if its neighboring countries were not able to do the same. Our world is so interconnected that global health and well-being cannot possibly be sustained if countries or people act alone. Instead, we must form global partnerships capable of protecting the vulnerable members of our global society.

[5] Have you ever heard of the term "One Health"? It means that the health of people, animals, and the environment are all interconnected as one. In other words, in order to protect our planet's health, we must recognize the "holistic partnership" between humans, animals, and ecosystems. Looking ahead to the post-COVID-19 world, we must ask ourselves some critical questions: What kind of partnerships will we need to create in the future? What role will each of us play in our interconnected global society? Our answers to these questions, and the actions we take, **determine** whether we will be able to create a peaceful and safe world full of hope for generations to come.

Check Your Understanding

Answer the following questions about the Reading Passage.

1. What is an example of how fear and anxiety made the situation worse during the COVID-19 pandemic?

2. What does "One Health" mean?

3. According to the passage, why do illnesses like COVID-19 spread more quickly and further afield than ever before?
   a. A virus cannot be prevented by people wearing masks and washing their hands.
   b. Our world has become a "global sphere" in which everything, including diseases, can travel quickly over borders.
   c. Illnesses are spread more quickly by animals than they are by humans.
   d. There are more vulnerable people in society than ever before.

4. According to the passage, which of the following statements describes the importance of making "global partnerships"? (*You can circle more than one correct answer.*)
   a. It's important to work together to produce new products to boost the global economy.
   b. Everything in our world is interconnected, so we cannot make a lasting change unless we include everyone.
   c. A partnership between, say, Japan and China will be good for the national economies of both countries.
   d. If we don't work together, feelings of fear and anxiety will divide us and create barriers between us.

Vocabulary Review

Fill in the blanks with the words from the box below. Change the form of the words if necessary.

pandemic	**sphere**	**exception**	**partnership**	**significance**
anxiety	**hoard**	**descent**	**desperate**	**determine**

1. The discovery of the new painting was of great ____________________ to art historians.
2. After the earthquake, many people ____________________ items like toilet paper and bottled water.
3. Many university students felt ____________________ during the economic downturn because they were unsure if they would be able to get jobs after graduation.
4. Many Brazilians of Japanese ____________________ have come to Japan to work and earn money.
5. People have the right to make their own choices in order to ____________________ their own futures.
6. Every country on the planet, without ____________________, must join the movement against climate change.
7. The situation in hospitals during the pandemic was ____________________. There were not enough medical supplies for everyone that needed them.

Listening Comprehension

Listen to two students having a conversation on an Internet video conferencing platform. Use the words in the box below to complete the summary of the conversation.

DL 29

Sally and James are both feeling tired of 1.________________________ during the pandemic. Sally wishes there was more that she could do 2.________________________. James mentions that he saw a news story about how medical workers are 3.________________________ and stressed, so he wants to encourage them somehow. Sally suggests making a social media page to promote the sending of 4.________________________ to local health care workers. Sally then suggests forwarding the social media page to their 5.________________________. They decide to 6.________________________ on it today.

classmates	**feeling exhausted**	**wearing masks**
staying home	**to help**	**positive messages**
get started	**teachers**	**donations**

17 PARTNERSHIPS FOR THE GOALS

SDG 17: Partnerships

The final goal of the SDGs is to form global partnerships. Everything in our world is interconnected. So, without global partnerships, we cannot fully solve any global issues. These global partnerships are not limited to countries. Rather, it is just as important that individuals form diverse partnerships.

Looking to the Future

If you could add one more goal to the SDGs, what would you add? With whom would you like to cooperate to achieve your new goal? Write a few sentences to explain your thoughts and discuss them with a partner.

Keywords:

Refugees LGBT+ One Health Relative Poverty Ethical Consumption

Clean Energy Insect Food Flexitarian Child Labor Food Waste Water Scarcity

Animal Welfare Plastic Free Virtual Water Climate Crisis Compassion

Friends

Family

Teachers

People of the world

Others

My reaction

Action Create and Share Your Own SDGs Project

In this textbook, we have learned about various global issues and some of the ways in which the SDGs aim to solve them. For our final activity, select one SDGs-related issue and make an action plan to be continued for one year from today. Go to page 117 for details.

SDGs Quick Quiz

Can you guess the answer to the following SDGs-related question? Test your knowledge.

According to the 2020 "Sustainable Development Report," what is Japan's ranking out of 166 countries in terms of achieving the SDGs?

a. 5th b. 17th c. 35th d. 87th

Check your answer on page 117.

Chapter 1 Action Worksheet

Getting to Know the SDGs

Step 1 Look at each of the seventeen SDGs below and divide them into three groups: *Environment*, *Society*, and *Economy*. There is no single correct answer, so use your imagination.

Environment	Society	Economy

Step 2 Share your opinion with a partner.

Step 3 Select three of the SDGs that interest you the most and write down why you chose them. Then get into small groups and share your opinion.

Step 4 Of the different ideas you heard in this activity, which one(s) are you the most interested in ? Why?

Quick Quiz Answer: d

Chapter 2 Action Worksheet

What Can We Do to Tackle Climate Change?

Step 1 Use the columns below to make a list of the things we can do in our daily lives to help prevent climate change. Next to each action, briefly explain WHY it's good for the environment.

Examples:

Action	Why is it good for the environment?
Turning off the lights when you leave a room	Electricity production emits CO_2, so, by saving electricity, we reduce CO_2 emissions.
Eating locally produced foods	Locally produced foods don't need to be transported as far, so less CO_2 is emitted by trucks.

My list:

Action	Why is it good for the environment?

Step 2 Share your ideas with a partner.

Step 3 Get into small groups. Then select your top three ideas and present them to your class.

Step 4 Of the different ideas you heard about during this activity, which one will you act upon first? Why?

Chapter 3 Action Worksheet

Checking Our Water Use

Step 1 Use the table below to keep track of how much water you use over the course of an average day. At the end of the day, calculate the total number of liters you used.

Category	Volume of Water Used	Number of Times	Subtotal
Laundry (1 load)	120 liters*		
Cooking / dish cleaning (1 meal)	60 liters*		
Bath (1 full tub)	200 liters*		
Shower (5 minutes)	60 liters		
Toilet (1 flush)	10 liters		
Washing hands (20 seconds)	4 liters		
Brushing teeth (30 seconds)	6 liters		
Other (watering, cleaning)	12 liters**		
		Total:	

* *Divide the number of liters by the number of people living in your household.*
** *Running water from a faucet for 1 minute uses about 12 liters of water.*

Step 2 Share your list with a partner.

Step 3 In small groups, share your water-use calculations from Step 1 and brainstorm ways to reduce water use in the different categories.

Category	Our ideas to reduce water use

Step 4 Choose your top three ideas and present them to the class.

Did you know?
According to the World Health Organization (WHO), the minimum amount of water required for a single human is 50 liters a day. The average person in Japan uses about 286 liters of water a day.

Quick Quiz Answer: b

Chapter 4 Action Worksheet

Imagining the Future of Energy

Step 1 Imagine life in 2050. How will we be using renewable energy sources in our daily lives? Use your imagination and brainstorm different creative ways in which we may be using renewable energy in the future.

> *Tip: It's okay if your ideas seem silly or unrealistic! Just let your mind wander and think of as many creative, interesting ideas as you can!

Step 2 Choose your favorite idea from Step 1 and draw a picture describing it in the space below. Then prepare a brief explanation of your idea. After you have finished, share it with a partner.

Example:

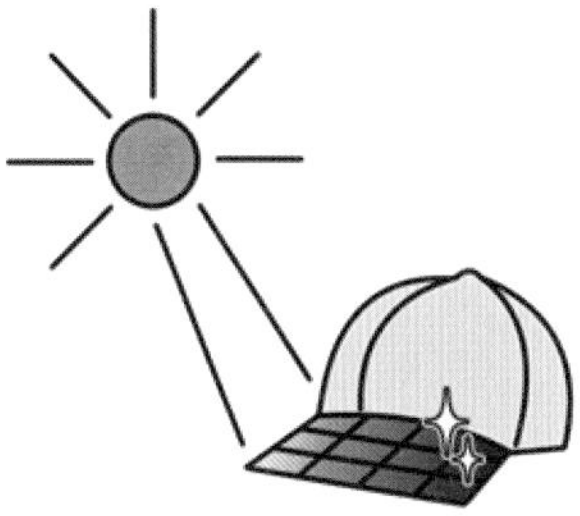

"In 2050, I think our hats will have solar panels on them so that we can power our smartphone and other devices when we go out."

My drawing:

My explanation:

Step 3 Walk around the classroom and share your idea with other classmates.

Chapter 5 Action Worksheet

World Food Distribution

Step 1 As a group, divide your items among your group members. It doesn't matter how you divide the items as long as your group agrees.

Step 2 Explain to the class how your group distributed its items. Then think about which of the four categories each group represents (*developed*, *emerging*, *developing*, or *least developed*).

Step 3 Distribute the items among the four groups. Discussion and the exchange of items between groups are allowed. *Importantly, consider that any two items represent a sufficient amount of food for one person.*

Step 4 Answer the following questions and share your thoughts with the class.

1. How do you feel about the share of items that you received? Do you think the items were shared equally? Why or why not?

2. Could everyone in the world get enough food if it were fairly distributed? Why or why not?

3. Based on this activity, what do you think is the most important thing needed to solve world poverty?

Quick Quiz Answer: b

Chapter 6 Action Worksheet

Reducing Our Food Waste

Step 1 Make a list of all of the food you throw away in the course of a single week. Use the list below as an example. In the "Reason" column, write a number according to the following:

① There was too much food, so I couldn't eat it all.
② There was something I didn't like or can't eat in it.
③ It didn't taste good.
④ It was past its expiration date.
⑤ It was past its "best by" date.
⑥ Other reason (write in yourself)

Food name	How much did I throw away?	Day of the week	Reason
(Ex.) Rice	*¼ bowl*	*Monday*	①
(Ex.) Milk	*¼ carton*	*Tuesday*	④
(Ex.) Tomato	*1 slice*	*Tuesday*	⑥ *I dropped it on the floor*

*Tip: Don't confuse "best by" date and expiration date. They are not the same. Keep this in mind when you are trying to reduce food waste.

"best by" date ≠ expiration date

Step 2 Share your list with a partner.

Step 3 In groups, brainstorm different ways to reduce food loss. Try to be as creative as possible.

Examples:

- *If your lunch box contains more food than you can eat, give some to a friend.*
- *Make a "food expiration" calendar and put it on the refrigerator.*

Step 4 Choose your top three ideas and briefly present them to the class.

Quick Quiz Answer: a (overweight), c (obese)

Chapter 7 Action Worksheet

Cause and Effect Chain

Step 1 Carefully read the ten cards below. Each card contains a negative situation that may be a reason for a child not getting an education.

Cards:

★ Can't go to school	A. Low income	B. Not enough skills to work	C. Can't buy enough food	D. No stable source of income
E. Get sick easily	F. Can't get enough nutrition	G. Can't read or write	H. Adult not able to work	I. Children have to work

Step 2 Together with a partner, use the cards to make a negative chain of events. Consider the connection between each card. The card that says, "Cannot go to school" should be the first card in the chain.

Example:

★ Can't go to school	→	G. Can't read or write	→		→		→	
↑								↓
I. Children have to work	←		←		←		←	

*Tip: Note that there is no right or wrong answer to this activity. This reflects the fact that there are many complex reasons for a child not getting an education.

Step 3 Make a group with another pair of classmates. Explain your completed chain to them.

Step 4 Answer the following questions. Then discuss your answers in your groups.

1. From among the reasons mentioned on the cards, what do you think are the most common reasons why children in poorer countries cannot go to school?

2. If you were caught up in such a negative sequence of events, do you think you would be able to escape on your own? Why or why not?

3. What do you think children in poorer countries need to be able to escape from this negative chain?

Quick Quiz Answer: d

Chapter 8 Action Worksheet

Beyond Gender Stereotypes

Step 1 Read the headings in each of the spaces below. Write your reaction to each of them in the spaces provided. (You will share this later, so don't write about anything you don't want to talk about.)

Things you like doing that are often expected of your gender

Things you don't like doing that are often expected of your gender

Things we need to do in order to achieve gender equality for everyone

Things you like doing that are often expected of the other genders

Things you don't like doing that are often expected of the other genders

Step 2 Share your ideas with a partner.

Step 3 Walk around the classroom and share your ideas with your classmates.

Step 4 In small groups, discuss the following questions.

1. Do you have any new insights into your own gender stereotypes? What are they?
2. Do you feel traditional gender stereotypes are true? Why or why not?
3. What can we do to promote gender equality for all members of our society, including the LGBT community?

Quick Quiz Answer: c

Chapter 9 Action Worksheet

Where Do You Belong?

Step 1 Close your eyes and wait quietly for your teacher to put a dot sticker on your forehead.

Step 2 Walk around the classroom and make groups based on the stickers. You shouldn't speak or even move your mouth. When you have finished making your group, sit down together. The activity will end after everyone has sat down.

Step 3 Remove your sticker and look at it. Then answer the questions below.

1. How did you feel after joining a group? Or, if you couldn't join a group, how did you feel?

2. Did you find your group quickly, or did it take time? How did you find your group?

3. What did you do when you noticed someone else having difficulty joining a group? Was there anything you could do to help them?

Step 4 Answer the following question and share your answer with the class.

If you were to do this activity again with the goal of making as big a group as possible, what would you do differently?

Quick Quiz Answer: d

Chapter 10 Action Worksheet

Insects and Memories from Childhood

Step 1 Close your eyes and stay quiet and still. Try to clear your mind and concentrate only on your breathing. Think about some positive memories from when you were a child that involve insects and bugs.

Step 2 Use the space below to draw a picture or write any words relating to your memories.

*Tip: You can include anything that you remembered, such as sights, sounds, and smells.

Step 3 Answer the following questions. Then share your answers with a partner.

1. Where and when did your memories take place?

2. What were you doing with the insects? Was there anyone else with you?

3. Are these memories important to you? Why or why not?

Step 4 Walk around the classroom and share your drawing and your memories with other classmates.

Quick Quiz Answer: d

Chapter 11 Action Worksheet

Making Advertisements

Step 1 Get into small groups and make a creative poster advertisement based on your topic card.

Step 2 Prepare a short presentation based on your poster. Read the topic card aloud and explain the content of your poster to the class, including any special meanings given to words, colors, or pictures.

Step 3 Think about the activity and how it made you feel. Answer the following questions and share your feelings and ideas with the class.

1. How did you feel while listening to the different messages in your classmates' presentations?

2. Which message in support of animal welfare was the most impressive to you? Why?

3. There can be many differing opinions about any given issue. How can we form our own opinions without being influenced by media and advertising?

Quick Quiz Answer: c (vegetarians), d (flexitarians)

Chapter 12 Action Worksheet

Plastic Waste Campaign

Step 1 Make a list of everyday products that are made of plastic. Look at the example below and similarly indicate which items are necessary (○), not really necessary (△), or not at all necessary (×). Then suggest how to reduce or eliminate your plastic waste.

Example:

Plastic items	Necessary/ Unnecessary?	How could you reduce or eliminate waste?
PET bottles from vending machines	×	Carry water in my own washable bottle
Plastic pens	△	Buy a long-lasting refillable pen instead of disposable ones
Plastic in my car	○	Consider buying a car that uses recycled plastic

My list:

Plastic items	Necessary/ Unnecessary?	How could you reduce or eliminate waste?

Step 2 Share your list with a partner.

Step 3 Get into small groups and share your list with your classmates. As a group, choose one plastic item from the list and plan a campaign encouraging people to reduce or rethink their use of this particular item.

Example campaign themes:

- **Campaign to encourage the use of washable drink bottles**
- **Campaign to promote one day a week as "no single-use plastic day"**

Step 4 Present your campaign to the class.

Quick Quiz Answer: d

Chapter 13 Action Worksheet

Buying It Forward

Step 1 Answer the following questions and share your answers with a partner.

If you could buy any one thing for yourself, what would you buy? Explain your choice. Roughly how much would it cost?

Step 2 Your task is to buy something for someone else that he or she needs. You must spend the same amount of money as you spent on the item you chose in Step 1. Think about what you would buy and why. Share your answer with your partner.

Price of my item in Step 1: ______________________________

What I would buy and why: ______________________________

____

Step 3 In a small group, brainstorm possible ways to spend your money in a manner consistent with the principles of ethical consumption. Think about three things: Who or what will you spend your money on? How will you spend your money (what will you buy)? Why?

Who/What?	How?	Why?
Example: *People suffering from poverty*	*By buying fair trade coffee*	*I like coffee, so I would like to support the people in other countries who work hard to produce it.*

Step 4 Present your group's best idea to the class.

Chapter 14 Action Worksheet

Create and Share Your Own SDGs Project

Step 1 Before you decide on a specific action plan, take some time to brainstorm possible SDGs-related issues that you might be able to focus on for your project.

Example:

SDGs-related Issues	Possible Action(s)
• *Plastic waste (SDG 11, 12, 14)*	• *Create a poster campaign at my school to encourage students to reduce plastic bottle use.*

Step 2 Share your ideas with a partner. Then choose one for your project and complete the following action plan.

My Project Name: ______________________________

How does your plan relate to the SDGs? (Related SDG Number ________)
What is the goal of your plan?
What specific actions will you need to take to complete your plan and achieve your goal? Include a timeline for each action.
With whom will you work on your project?

Step 3 Form a pair with another student and take two minutes each to explain your plans to each other. Then take a final two minutes in which to share any final opinions or questions about each other's projects.

Step 4 Repeat Step 3 several times with different partners and use their feedback to improve your project. If possible, try to find a partner with a similar project.

Quick Quiz Answer: b

Useful Links

The following websites are directly related to each of this textbook's fourteen chapters. These links are meant to complement the content and serve as extra resources for possible extension activities.

Chapter 1: Global Perspectives

Japan Ministry of Foreign Affairs—SDGs Indicators
(Japanese) https://www.mofa.go.jp/mofaj/gaiko/oda/sdgs/statistics/index.html

Learning for Global Citizens—Kazuya Oseki's Home Page（著者 HP）
*1 (Japanese) http://www.tokiwa.ac.jp/~oseki/

*1

Chapter 2: Climate Change

World Wildlife Foundation (WWF)—Global Warming
(Japanese) https://www.wwf.or.jp/activities/basicinfo/40.html?gclid

Fridays for Future
*2 (English) https://fridaysforfuture.org (Japanese) https://fridaysforfuture.jp

*2

Chapter 3: Water

World Health Organization (WHO)—Drinking Water
(English) https://www.who.int/news-room/fact-sheets/detail/drinking-water

Japan Ministry of the Environment—Virtual Water
*3 (Japanese) https://www.env.go.jp/water/virtual_water/

*3

Chapter 4: Clean Energy

The Renewable Energy Institute—Clean Energy
*4 (English) https://www.renewable-ei.org/en/ (Japanese) https://www.renewable-ei.org

Renewable Energy Policy Network for the 21st Century (REN21)—Renewables 2020 Global Status Report.
(English) https://www.ren21.net/wp-content/uploads/2019/05/gsr_2020_full_report_en.pdf

*4

Chapter 5: Poverty

Oxfam—The Power of People against poverty
(English) https://www.oxfam.org/en (Japanese) http://oxfam.jp/

Musubie—Kodomo Shokudo
*5 (Japanese) https://musubie.org

*5

Chapter 6: Hunger

World Food Programme (WEP) — Zero Hunger
(English) https://www.wfp.org/zero-hunger?_ga (Japanese) https://ja.wfp.org/zero-hunger

Second Harvest Japan—Foodbanks
*6 (Japanese) http://2hj.org/problem/foodbank/

*6

Chapter 7: Children

UNICEF—For Every Child
(English) https://www.unicef.org/ *7 (Japanese) https://www.unicef.or.jp/index.html

Save the Children
(English) https://www.savethechildren.net/ (Japanese) https://www.savechildren.or.jp/

*7

Chapter 8: Gender

World Economic Forum—Gender Gap Report 2020
(English) https://www.weforum.org/reports/gender-gap-2020-report-100-years-pay-equality

Plan International—The Because I'm a Girl Movement
(Japanese) https://www.plan-international.jp/girl/ *8 (English) https://plan-international.org/because-i-am-a-girl

*8

Chapter 9: Refugees

United Nations High Commissioner for Refugees (UNHCR)—Refugees
(English) https://www.unhcr.org (Japanese) https://www.unhcr.org/jp/

The Japan Association for Refugees—Fleeing for One's Life
*9 (Japanese) https://www.refugee.or.jp/refugee/

*9

Chapter 10: Insects

Green Facts—Biodiversity and Human Well Being

(English) https://www.greenfacts.org/en/biodiversity/index.htm#1 *10

The Honeybee Conservancy—Ten Ways to Save the Bees

*10 (English) https://thehoneybeeconservancy.org/how-to-save-the-bees/

Chapter 11: Vegetarianism

Japan Vegetarian Society—Vegetarianism

*11 (Japanese) http://www.jpvs.org/ *11

Animal Rights Center—Animal Welfare

(Japanese) https://arcj.org/

Chapter 12: Plastic Waste

World Wildlife Foundation (WWF)—How Does Plastic End Up in the Ocean?

(English) https://www.wwf.org.uk/updates/how-does-plastic-end-ocean *12

World Wildlife Foundation (WWF)—Plastic Waste

*12 (Japanese) https://www.wwf.or.jp/activities/basicinfo/3776.html?gclid

Chapter 13: Shopping

Ecological Footprint Calculator—Ecological Footprint

*13 (English) https://www.footprintcalculator.org *13

Fairtrade Japan / Fairtrade International—Fairtrade

(Japanese) https://www.fairtrade-jp.org / (English) https://www.fairtrade.net

Chapter 14: Partnerships

The Partnering Initiative (TPI)—SDGs Partnerships

(English) https://www.local2030.org/library/501/Maximising-the-impact-of-partnerships-for-the-SDGs-A-practical-guide-to-partnership-value-creation.pdf

Centers for Disease Control and Prevention(CDC)—One Health *14

*14 (English) https://www.cdc.gov/onehealth/index.html

Section Introduction Quotations

UN (2015) Transforming Our World: The 2030 Agenda for Sustainable Development.

https://www.un.org/ga/search/view_doc.asp?symbol=A/RES/70/1&Lang=E

Severn Cullis-Suzuki (1992) Speech at Rio Summit 1992.

*15 https://www.youtube.com/watch?v=T9YaagLB5Fg (UNIC Tokyo) *15

UN (1987) Our Common Future.

https://sustainabledevelopment.un.org/content/documents/5987our-common-future.pdf

UNESCO (1996) Learning: The Treasure Within — Report to UNESCO of the International Commission on Education for the Twenty-first Century.

https://www.eccnetwork.net/sites/default/files/media/file/109590engo.pdf (highlights)

UNESCO (2014) Global Citizenship Education: Preparing Learners for the Challenges of the 21st Century.

https://unesdoc.unesco.org/ark:/48223/pf0000227729

G. Pike & D. Selby (1999) In the Global Classroom 1, Toronto: Pippin Publishing.

Image Credits

Ms. Satsuki Yamagata: Inner Cover (Global Citizens Tree), Table of Contents (Butterflies and Leaves), Section Introductions (Flower Images), Icons for Headings and Page Numbers

Ms. Ayano Uchiyama: Reading Preview (Chapters 1, 2, 4, 7, 10, and 13); Action and Activities (Chapters 3, 4, 10, 11, and 12)

Living as Global Citizens [B-931]
An Introduction to the Sustainable Development Goals
地球市民として生きる：英語で学ぶ SDGs 実践入門

第1刷 2021年4月1日
第6刷 2023年9月25日

著 者	小関 一也 Kazuya Oseki ケビン マクマナス Kevin M. McManus
発行者	南雲 一範 Kazunori Nagumo
発行所	株式会社 南雲堂 〒162-0801 東京都新宿区山吹町361 NAN'UN-DO Co., Ltd. 361 Yamabuki-cho, Shinjuku-ku, Tokyo 162-0801, Japan 振替口座 : 00160-0-46863 TEL: 03-3268-2311（営業部：学校関係） 03-3268-2384（営業部：書店関係） 03-3268-2387（編集部） FAX: 03-3269-2486
編集者	堀田 華／伊藤 宏実
組 版	柴崎 利恵
装 丁	銀月堂
イラスト	山形 彩月
検 印	省 略
コード	ISBN978-4-523-17931-3 C0082

Printed in Japan

E-mail : nanundo@post.email.ne.jp
URL : https://www.nanun-do.co.jp/